**ANCHOR BOOKS**

ECHOES IN LIFE

Edited by

Steve Twelvetree

First published in Great Britain in 2004 by
ANCHOR BOOKS
Remus House,
Coltsfoot Drive,
Peterborough, PE2 9JX
Telephone (01733) 898102

All Rights Reserved

Copyright Contributors 2003

SB ISBN 1 84418 302 5

FOREWORD

Anchor Books is a small press, established in 1992, with the aim of promoting readable poetry to as wide an audience as possible.

We hope to establish an outlet for writers of poetry who may have struggled to see their work in print.

The poems presented here have been selected from many entries, and as always editing proved to be a difficult task.

I trust this selection will delight and please the authors and all those who enjoy reading poetry.

Steve Twelvetree
Editor

CONTENTS

Flames In The Sky	Phillip Tinsley	1
The Insane King	George S Johnstone	2
Restaurant View	John Lawrence	4
Love Is A Many Splendid Thing	Brian Conaghan	6
In Sickness And In Health	Don Goodwin	7
A Picture Of Memories	Kate Crowder	8
First Impressions	R Martin	10
It Takes Two	Mandy Jayne Moon	11
Untitled	Shirley Longford	12
The Shadow Of The Oak	Ian C Gray	13
The Fishermen	Geraldine McMullan Doherty	14
King Of The Sky	J Moorton	16
A Prayer	J Johnston	17
Bliss House, Washington, DC	Anthony M Blackwell	18
La Crème De La Crème	June Howard Elias	19
Who's Driving Ambition?	Steve Beckles-Ebusua	20
Prayer Line	Hazel Mills	22
The Autumn	Janet Brook	23
The Warrior	Stephen Frederick Burns	24
Jealousy	Hannah Kennington	25
Jane Louise	B Foster	26
Which Path To Take	Jeanette Gaffney	27
Alien Advice	Anthony G L Kent	28
Charter Flights	Bill Looker	29
The Light For All	Rose Mills	30
We Can Choose	Rosemary Davies	31
The Cut	J Lodge	32
Did I Step On A Cowslip?	Ian Bowen	33
Hallowe'en Fear	Margaret B Baguley	34
Myth	M Morris	35
Feis Na Samhna	Paul Birkett	36
Hallowe'en	Michael D Bedford	37
The Piano Player	David Charman	38
Driving	June Melbourn	39
A Giving Heart	Gill Gardner	40

Never Stop Believing	Pauline Bloomfield	41
Wot	Persi-Vere	42
Games	Ricky N Lock	43
Rivington Views	Laird P Brewer	44
To The Naked Eye	Emma Scott	45
Angel On The Sidewalk	Karen Smith	46
Peter Kay	Anne Sackey	47
Serves You Right!	Jacqueline O'nions	48
Live Your Dreams	G Siddall	49
Our Children	Jean-Angela Smith	50
Halcyon Days (Nottinghamshire)	Mary Skelton	51
The Man In The Moon	May Ward	52
Childhood	Emma Scott	53
Call Him Ted	Dean Riches	54
A Mortgage, Credit Card	David M Walford	56
Night	F R Smith	57
Wake-Up Call	Greta Robinson	58
Free And Easy	Lyn Sandford	59
War Is Not For Me	Dennis L Vasey	60
The Fog	Lorraine Noble	61
Possible Dreams	Joan Prentice	62
Ode To Seraphim	C Thornton	63
Fireworks Day	Alan Pow	64
Driving Through Menna	Roland Gurney	65
My Sin	A F Mace	66
Far-Thing	Nick Clifton	67
The Snow	Geoffrey Leech	68
Paradise	Megan Strong	69
Relaxing	Heather Moore	70
A Canal Life	Bridie Sutton	71
Purpose Of Life	Jean Hargreaves	72
Dream On	Mary McKeeve Moore	73
The Fourteen Million To One Chance	George Petrie	74
The Curtain Shop	Patricia Samuels	75
USA 1997	Anthony Sherman	76
Frantic	Chris Needley	77

Lover's Memories	Tom Spencer	78
Darkness Embrace Me	A Vellam	79
Summer Holidays	C M Thompson	80
Dusty Dreams	Joy Pearson	82
Who Am I, Friend?	C R Slater	84
Messages	Vann Scytere	85
Hail To Thee 'The Enemy'		
All's Fair In Love And Jaw! It!	E J Williams	86
	John L Wright	87
The Anglers	Linda Ross	88
My God	Denise Shaw	89
Merchant Of Your Dreams	Carol Olson	90
Limericks	Charlotte J Ireson	91
The Shopping Trolley Two-Step	Gatekeeper	92
Your Big Mistake!	Emma J Riddin	93
Grey	Denise Place	94
You're My Everything	Anna Yates	96
Lack Of Foresight	Lachlan Taylor	97
Nursery Rhymes	D R Thomas	98
I'll Say A Quiet Prayer	Peter Wesley Hayward	100
Innocence Lost	Frances Ridett	101
Moonlight	Melanie Rowe	102
Below There!	A I B Vaughan	103
People	Mary O'Connell	104
Why Poetry?	Alan Wilson	106
One Night!	Helen Trevatt	107
Seasons	James Patrick Milton	108
Into The Red Sky	Joe Wood	109
The Greatest Show On Earth	Brian L Porter	110
At First I Looked Down On You, But Now You . . .	John Waby	112
The Midnight Carousel	Jonathan Pegg	114
The Quiet Scene	Terry Daley	115
Lost My Bottle	Carol Hanney	116
The Fire Demon	Peter W Hodgkins	117
Look At Me!	Rowena	118
Forbidden As He Is	C Hansbury	119

Washday	Muriel Johnson	120
Sorry	Maria Jenkinson	121
Oh To Be An Angel	L Alan Johnson	122
The Chiropractor	Marilyn Hine	123
Slave Ship	David Kolodynski	124
Our Village Green	Doreen Lawrence	125
Summertime	J T Lister	126
Food For Thought	T G Bloodworth	127
Domestic Violence	Jennifer Austin	128
Unrequited Love	Stephanie Abberley	129
Lonely Tears	Matthew L Burns	130
Horatio Vincta	M J Banasko	131
Icons	Norman Bissett	132
Next Time	Sheila Benard	133
The Fan	Helen Carpenter	134
Is There A Choice?	Stan Coombs	135
Footing The Bill	Hilary J Cairns	136
Alter Ego	Anthony Brady	137
Beautiful As You Are	Gordon Barnett	138
Home, Tweet Home?	Sue Coles	139
Bless Our Days	C S Cyster	140
Images II (Azania)	Victor Church	141
Where Is Heaven?	Stephanie Cox	142
A-Z Of Animals	Mrinalini Dey	143
Divorce	Carol Davies	144
Somebody's Calling	John Faucett	145
A Day At The Seaside	L Fritchley	146
Celebrity Status	Jack Edwards	147
Backstage	Stephen Friede	148
Thinking	Julie Wiles	149
The Day That You Left Me	Alison Mayo	150
Star-Stricken	Chris Gutteridge	151
The Hatchling	Ellen Chambers	152
Change The Chains That Bind	Rosie Hues	153
Who Loves - Wins	Mark Musgrave	154
My Guarded Secret	Joan Craven	155
Facing The Future	Susan Haldenby	156

Rock 'N' Roll	Brian Lunt	157
Pain	Sharon Simpson	158
Wherever There's A Mother	Marion Schoeberlein	159
A Sudden Storm	Eddie Main	160
The Lucky Horseshoe	James Ayrey	161

FLAMES IN THE SKY

Down the runway Concorde roared
Thundering on with all aboard
Excitement in the pounding heart
Wings outspread, a silver dart

Supersonic elegance poise and grace
Atlantic flight with time will race
To soar towards the stratosphere
All destinations are so near

Lifting slightly from the ground
Flames and smoke were all around
A plume of fire trailed behind
With thick black smoke, the choking kind

Panic as the seconds pass
Abject terror in first class
Poignant footage of the flight
Going down an awful sight

Flying in a blazing stream
People in a ghastly dream
Slow motion feelings, words unsaid
A sickening crash and all are dead.

Phillip Tinsley

THE INSANE KING

His throne was made from broken glass
On his head a crown of beads,
The robe that ill-fitted him is in tatters
For fun he grew sunflower seeds.

Until after eleven he would daily slumber
Then get up for tripe and peas,
He would take a bubble bath standing up
As he only washed his knees.

His favourite card game was rouge-et-noir
Funny that he always won,
But then who would have dared beat him
To lose your head is no fun.

One day per month he would hold court
To learn how his kingdom fared,
His advisors would tell him all was well
To tell the truth, they were scared.

Every midnight he would take a stroll
Around the grand palace garden,
Sometimes he would bump into a tree
And say 'I beg your pardon.'

At other times, he would walk sideways
With slippers on the wrong feet,
His breeches he always wore inside out
Because he thought it neat.

Queen Grizelda always nagged at him
For eating with just a spoon,
She said it wasn't befitting for a king
To act like a big buffoon.

Civil etiquette bored the sovereign silly
Especially with those foreign guests,
Them to backwards speak always would he
That really confused the pests.

He played the harpsichord rather poorly
His singing was just as bad,
But no one dared tell him otherwise
In case it got him mad.

His ministerial aides tried to oust him
On more than one occasion,
They are now banished from the realm
On permanent vacation!

The people said the king was insane
And not competent to rule,
But the king wasn't bothered by this
He knew he wasn't such a fool.

The king did all this stuff deliberately
That way he was left alone,
He is not the fool that people think
He still sits on the throne.

George S Johnstone

Restaurant View

Cream marble statues
Take sight in my mind
Trotting shoes, black,
Striking lightning
On the Italian marble floor.
A twist and a turn of direction:
She goes east, west, south, north
In one turn.
She doesn't travel the globe.

Orange-juice sky,
Pyramid-shaped leaves,
In visible branches -
Just an almond twig,
Fading away in the distance.
Stone grey rooftops.
Dirt-mushroomed pigeons
Race their unknown circuit.

Luminous orange lamps
Will shortly light up

When the sun, a peach,
Goes back in the cupboard.

The fizzed Coke
Sparkles and fizzes my throat.
Looking-in thoughts
Run deep.
Beige varnished bar, curves
Colliding with cream
Flowered wallpaper.
Sunken cushion
Sinking my back.

Orange peach fights back
In the coated blue cupboard

Of the sky, whose clouds
Cushion fragile minds.

John Lawrence

LOVE IS A MANY SPLENDID THING

He asked me:
'What do you think about love?'

I said:
'Love, love, love, *mmm*, let me see,
Love is:
A monkey swinging you from a tree
A bear clawing at your guts
A parasite dining on your desires
A snake squeezing the goodness from your bones
A rat gnawing at your every emotion
A cat squealing in your fragile ear
A butterfly fluttering circles in your soul
A wolf howling around your mind
A herd stampeding through your heart.'

'That's a cynical view of love.' He said
'I know.' I said
'You must have had some pretty grim experiences.' He said
'Not at all, the women in my life have all been incredible beasts.' I said

He left soon after
wishing
he'd never asked
the damn
polluted question.

And I wished I'd never answered it!

Brian Conaghan

IN SICKNESS AND IN HEALTH

They took their vows in church to stay together in sickness
and in health,
Everything was going fine at first, while he still had his wealth,
But then his illness started slowly at first in the early days,
Now he is in a wheelchair and the bills he cannot pay.
Now his wife has left him, so much for the vows 'in sickness
and in health'.
They would still have been together if he had still got his
faculties and, of course, his wealth.

Don Goodwin

A Picture Of Memories

I love you truly, I always will
A picture of childhood memories
I cherish still.

Playing games of Two-Ball at my gran's
Waiting for the man
Who sold Salt 'n' Shake crisps
On his greengrocery van.

Going for walks with Grandad
Down the quarries, fun times we had
Up humps, down hollows
We were never sad.

Trips down Folly there were many, in Kirkby shops, Landers,
                                                    Newcombes,
Me mam spent every penny
Working hard at weaving springs
Dad down pit working every hour God sent.

My childhood days of learning were filled with laughter 'n' fun
That Maypole dance at Morven Park School I had just done
The break time came with treats to buy,
'Two Jammie Dodgers, please,' I'd cry.

Our special supper treat came on Friday nights
That large black chippie van was a marvellous sight
Down the street went me mam, white basin in hand
Bringing back a large feast that was scrumptiously grand.

Now all grown up with kids of my own
Older 'n' wiser through things I have known
Taking a trip down Memory Lane
To the place of my childhood, but alas it's not the same.

My picture of memories
Brings a tear to my eye, a smile to my face
Remembering many cherished moments of *time* and *place*.

Kate Crowder

First Impressions

We never get a second chance to make a first impression,
So we must make our first impression really count,
Judgements will be made when people meet us for the first time,
So what they see could be regarded as paramount.

If we fail to make a good impression at the start,
It will be harder to convince people of our worth,
We must try to convince them at our first meeting,
That there is no better person on the Earth.

At the same time we should remember we are only as good as yesterday,
And the good first impression will be of no avail,
Unless that impression is constantly maintained,
It is certain that in the long run we will fail.

We cannot be successful in everything we do,
Otherwise there would be no winners in life's game,
What is important is that we always make an effort,
In this way the impression could always be the same.

If we always strive to make a good impression,
And do our best when conditions are adverse,
You can be sure that our efforts will be noticed,
And other people's reactions will not be perverse.

R Martin

IT TAKES TWO

He says he's working late tonight,
But something tells me this isn't right.
It's not just once or twice a week,
So is it a new love that he seeks?
When it comes to making love, I know it's not the same,
And while he was sleeping, he whispered someone's name.
This was a girl from work, as he's mentioned her before,
And when I try to talk to him, he heads right for the door.
I just can't bear the thought of both of them together,
As when I said those words 'I do', I thought it was forever.
When I sat him down, and said 'It's time to know,
Is it me, or is it her, which one of us will go?'
He told me he was sorry and with me he wants to stay,
So both of us are trying, and taking it day by day.

Mandy Jayne Moon

UNTITLED

Sleep, we all sleep,
Dream, we all dream,
Food, we have to eat,
Places, where we can meet,
Night, it gets dark,
The moon begins to shine,
Above us while we sleep,
We all sleep, we all dream,
We all do what it seems,

Love, we all love,
Someone in our lives,
Peace, do we get some peace?
Relax, that's what to do,
To get ourselves to sleep,
Recuperate from every day,
To send ourselves to dream,

Dream, dream, some of us dream,
Do you remember yours?
I can recall one or two,
From long ago, too.

Sleep, we all sleep,
Dream, we all dream.

Shirley Longford

THE SHADOW OF THE OAK

I rested 'neath the old gnarled oak
In the shadows of its bough
And I espied a traveller
Whose tale I tell here now.

At first he was the merest speck
As he crossed the vale below
And lost to the darkened forest
Where the fearless only go.

Then suddenly before me
He appeared from out the glare:
I had not seen him coming
And, a'feared, could only stare.

'Good morrow to you pilgrim'
I ventured forth to say
But the words I tried to utter
Did just dryly die away.

Behind him shone the brightest sun
And I strained my eyes to see;
What manner of a traveller
Could this haloed figure be.

I stood up there before him
Then was chilled through to the bone
For in the shadow of the oak
I was standing all alone!

Ian C Gray

THE FISHERMEN

The fishing boats are rocking
Across the blue lagoon
Bringing home the fishermen
Under the bright full moon.

They're looking towards the harbour
For a loved one waiting there
The boys are tired and hungry
Wondering does anyone care

The boats of different colours
With their lights glittering above
Their oilskins full of fish scales
And prawn stabs in their glove.

Other men are on the harbour
To give a willing hand
Getting their ropes together
To help each other land.

Husbands' wives grow anxious
With their babies all at home
Worried that their men are back
Across the Irish foam.

Paddy is a skipper
He's fished for many a year
He knows the tide inside out
This work he loves so dear.

What's that I see a'coming?
It's a boat, but what's the noise?
It's Paddy steering gently
Coming home with the boys.

Three crew come in all smiling
With their faces glowing red
Playing their favourite songs on board
It's Friday! And they'll get paid!

Geraldine McMullan Doherty

KING OF THE SKY

Sitting up here in the highest tree
King of the air and all I can see
I'm big and large with a big, hooked beak
For what I am I can't be weak
What is it I see down there?
Why, it's a great grizzly bear
He's sitting down there by the river
Watching the salmon spawn and shiver
Now he decides it's time to eat
And hooks one out with his great feet
He has his meal and then moves on
No one knows where he has gone
I sit and watch from my branch on high
Then decide I'll have a fly
I just take off and flap my wings
Then soar on high, watching things
I'll find a mate to have some chicks
But first I must find some sticks
To build a nest up in a tree
So all the world the chicks will see
I'm so graceful and look so regal
King of the sky 'cause I'm a Golden Eagle!

J Moorton

A Prayer

Dear Father,

Please teach me how to pray
Morning noon and night
To know that I am always in your sight.
When I pray out loud
I do not imagine you sitting on a cloud.
I feel your presence everywhere
Helping me with your loving care.
Help me to know how you would like me to be
And not to worry what people on Earth think of me.
You gave me blessings from above,
So to you, Lord, I send my love.

J Johnston

BLISS HOUSE, WASHINGTON, DC

A large cabaret with a pool at one end,
Rose trellises blocking the view.
They dressed for farewell: white suits, long gowns sequinned;
The Bliss House could not continue.

The party should have been for Armistice Day,
It took place the following spring.
This site had been seized for radio relay;
A crucial site for transmitting.

The party was gaudy and loud, with an edge,
The fine folk were strained by the news.
They had done their bit in the war, with courage;
Impossible, now, to refuse.

Concurrently, Europe monarchies crumbled,
Their fine folk were looted and shot.
Their properties seized, their dependants humbled,
Their rights, we now say, we forgot.

Some folk were not fine folk; we got a good look,
Sir Robber Baron, Doctor Mutes,
Those tied in with human experiment gook,
The advocates of substitutes.

We had to conclude: all is well, safely rest;
We strained to accept the unjust.
The Negro musicians stood waiting request;
Another war loomed, fight we must.

Anthony M Blackwell

LA CRÈME DE LA CRÈME

The long months of planning were over at last,
The dreams and the distance were things of the past,
In our ears was the music played by the Basque band
As we sat on a stone bench in Stade Colombe stand
Surrounded by Frenchmen we smiled, 'mon ami',
But we knew underneath it was 'l'enemi'.
The scene was forever set in remembrànce
Of the day that we shared in 'allez la Frànce'
Then after the anthem - the scene of the play.
Will red dragon or blue cock be victor today?
The Frenchmen were strong, determined and wild,
And we sweated and laboured like mothers in child.
The Welshmen fought back in a way so immense
By keeping the atmosphere thrilling and tense,
And despite all the pressure delivered their art
To the Frenchmen, and served them true Welsh 'à la carte'.
And then! It was over, the moment suprème
With the Gallois victorious, 'la crème de la crème'.

June Howard Elias

WHO'S DRIVING AMBITION?

Sardines on a busy train
Minds not geared for work
Their blank expressions and worn-out faces
Seems they're geared to reverse.

On entering work, first gear is set
The start-up for the day
Off in lanes, their nine to five
Ready, come what may.

First gear to second, work no end
It seems you're winning the race
But apathy cuts in, boredom arrives
Enthusiasm left no trace.

Tea break arrives, refuel time
A stop that is badly needed
But a dismal amount of quality work
A performance that cannot be repeated

Break time ends, restart time
Some engines keen and slick
But others cannot continue the pace
And decide to go off sick

Bellies and expression empty
As they queue for their lunchtime service
They're now in third gear motion
Which will recharge goals and purpose

Top gear is reached, no thought needed
For this mundane life of work
Photocopy last piece of project
Oh no, it's gone berserk!

Home time looms, it must be asked
What other route to take?
We're all caught up in the working highway
A trap that's hard to break.

But to drive on and forget your family and friends
You cannot be too brash
'Cause as you power, ahead in front
You may cause your fatal crash!

Steve Beckles-Ebusua

Prayer Line

Prayer for me is a telephone line
To someone who's listening all of the time
But often I find that it's hard to connect
And then all my prayers are suddenly wrecked.

So can I connect through this telephone line
And speak to the One who is there all the time?
Only if I can believe He is there;
Then life is no longer so barren and bare.

But how do I pay for this telephone bill
When I seem to have lost my faith and my will?
It cannot be paid for in silver and gold,
Not even with all of the money I hold.

But then, I just know that my telephone's free
And the One who will listen is waiting for me.
So all that I need is the faith just to pray
To someone I know, who forever will stay.

Hazel Mills

THE AUTUMN

The autumn is here,
Can't you tell?
The crisp breezes,
That you can smell.

The freshened winds,
That blow so strong,
Winter is coming,
It won't be long.

Slowly drifting,
From the clouds,
The pure white snow,
Lies on the ground.

The snows will lie,
Upon the ground,
The crispy crunching,
Of the footstep, sound.

The little robin,
Is in the tree,
You know it's winter,
When it's him you see.

Janet Brook

THE WARRIOR

I stand alone so proud
A warrior and a brave
Having vowed all my life
I will be no slave

The white man came, took all our land
Killed all the buffalo
Our land so full of promise
So very long ago

The white man killed the warriors
The woman and the child
In their eyes all white men saw
Were savages so wild!

No matter that we wanted peace
And offered them our hand
They took all our buffalo hide
And wanted more than land

The white man hunted night and day
'Til nearly all were gone
I stand alone so proud and pray
I'm not the only one

My brothers now, they all have gone
Their spirits have been broken
All the white man gave each one
Was a plot of land, a token?

Yes, in my heart I'll always be
A warrior and a brave
Because of this I will stay free
And never be a slave.

Stephen Frederick Burns

JEALOUSY

They tease you about your intelligence,
They hate the way you achieve,
They envy all your successes,
Your freedom, they try to seize,

Nasty comments,
Evil stares,
Hurtful barges,
Hateful glares,

They blackmail you, they often threaten,
They are the cause of all your screams,
Your biggest enemy 'the bullies'
Every night they haunt your dreams,

Killer threats,
Prepare to fight,
They hate you that much,
You won't live another night,

They are jealous of your appearance,
They want your caring ways,
They envy your beauty,
They say it's the innocent one who pays.

Hannah Kennington (15)

JANE LOUISE

Forty years ago today,
A precious bundle came my way,
Presented to me by my wife,
Someone I'll treasure all my life,
We called our little daughter, Jane,
She never caused us any pain,
I can't recall one day of stress,
Just countless hours of happiness,
She later then increased the prize,
At least I'm sure so in my eyes,
My two granddaughters blessed her marriage,
Something, no one can disparage,
And as I've watched all three mature,
There's one thing that I know for sure,
They will ever hold my pride of place,
Along with their grandmother, Grace,
Such a source of constant pleasure,
All of them my family treasure,
I know my love will not diminish,
I'll have them right until the finish.

Dad

B Foster

WHICH PATH TO TAKE

You never know
Which path to take
In life we have
To make mistakes
It's how we learn
To nurture grow
Where life takes on
A warmer glow
A baby comes
To give you joy
To share in all
You do and say
For life will always
Have its way
You move into
A different time
When now as parents
You will find
It's better than
It was before
And love will be there
At your door.

Jeanette Gaffney

ALIEN ADVICE

It lay completely still and silent
an awesome iridescent giant.
The huge craft's ramp began descending.
'Twas rusty, bent and needed mending.
But I found no cause for my alarm,
as one green being cried, 'We mean no harm.'

They said, 'We have Starcruiser
fit with new hi-fi and woofer.
Electrician gave a shriek
'All set up without a squeak.'

'Picked up transmission on the line
Of BBC 'Last Summer Wine'.
And that is how within a week
such perfect English we do speak.

'Foolish Earthlings know you make
a very stupid big mistake.
You really should have realised
how wrong is coming 'civilised'.

'We fear you creatures never will
learn respect all things, not kill.
You really in grave danger from
flipping great atomic bomb.

'You ought to take a lot more care
and learn not to pollute your air.
When approach your world, we say a prayer
for whopping hole in ozone layer.

'But greatest danger to mankind,'
they said, as Earth they left behind.
'It's not too late, advice to take,
Watch not 'Neighbours' for goodness sake!'

Anthony G L Kent

CHARTER FLIGHTS

In a fit of economy quite false
in a charter plane we flew
the intercom was all in Morse
and we queued at the outside loo!

The Tower gave the word to go
our captain takes a gamble
we taxi, ominously slow
and lift off in a scramble

The talk is all of duty-free
and rip-offs by the Dago
the pilot goes out for his tea
the in-flight meal is sago.

Bill Looker

THE LIGHT FOR ALL

A light that shines for all of us
It's here for always, just look and see
No matter if the light is hot or cold
Please have no fear and let it be.

The light leads the way to all joys
In no matter what place or times
If you need a helping hand
Just look for the light that shines.

That light shines within us all
Has been placed within you care
Giving its light to share with us all,
Because the light knows you're there.

Rose Mills

WE CAN CHOOSE

There is so much beauty on this Earth,
Fit for both king and peasant.
We need to protect the land of our birth,
Make sure it remains safe and pleasant.
We must always do our mortal best,
To stand up for what is right.
Upon our laurels we mustn't rest,
Even if it means there's a war to fight.
It's easy to turn a blind eye,
And pretend bad things aren't happening.
Until events make us question why?
Soon we will face the day of reckoning.
Do we realise what we stand to lose?
It's up to us because we can choose!

Rosemary Davies

THE CUT

Down by the cut on a summer morn,
Another day of tranquillity is born.
Narrow boat engines thud as they get underway,
Ready for cruising along the waterway.
Windlass in hand ready to work the lock,
No one ever worries about the clock.
Time stands still when you cruise the waterways,
For many it is a place where they will end their days.
No cars, or fumes, no speeding here and there.
The fast pace of life too much to bear.
Wildlife lives beneath the willow canopies.
Birds can be heard singing in the trees.
Ducks and swans paddle on by
There is not a cloud in the sky.
Colourful dragonflies go on their way.
Baby rabbits in the fields at play.
People walk their dogs along the towpaths.
Children ride their bikes having fun and laughs.
Narrow boats decked out in their traditional glory.
Castles and roses painted, tell a long-forgotten story.
Gone are the days when the working boats were all we saw
Now the pleasure boats cruise the canal taking a tour.
Life on the cut is such a peaceful scene
But for many, it is just a dream!

J Lodge

DID I STEP ON A COWSLIP?

Today
I walk
Retired
In nature's
Woods
And fields
Aware
Of world
Affairs
I tread
On
Unknown flora
With
Misspent pastoral
A
Modern man
In
An ancient
Garden
Naively unaware
Of
Nature's tags.

Ian Bowen

HALLOWE'EN FEAR

The night falls like a cloak
Around the house.
No moon, so dark and deep
Hallowe'en shadows move
More sinister and ever nearer
Creep silent and make us start
And furtively look
Over our shoulders
Afraid of what we'll see.
A face looms from the dark
And in the hall confronts us
'Who is there?'
And realise 'tis ourselves
In a mirror.

Margaret B Baguley

MYTH

Another year is over,
so soon the need to rise,
strange it is the physical
so unused am I to eyes.
This night beyond all others
is all I have to give,
a little pain is all I gain
but what it is to live.
To see the terror in their faces,
to feel their dread and fear,
stripping away their false illusions
as my presence becomes clear.
None fear me as a passing draught,
a chill upon the stair,
but a hundred nameless missing
alone could cry, 'Beware!'
One night only am I flesh,
one need alone sustains me,
to kill and feed and watch them bleed,
before once more the grave contains me.

M Morris

FEIS NA SAMHNA

Anticipation swells hazy autumn day, voices chant for dusk to fall
lunar calendar controls Druid ceremonies in earth-covered hall
life and death celebration, Samhain, Celtic feast of the dead
Samana the Leveller, Grim Reaper, feeds their primal dread
pagan worshippers duck for apples in nemeton, sacred groves
magic charms contact lost souls of Achren in frenzied droves
reading the future with witches' mirrors and nutshell ashes
cavorting figures dance in the spell of autumn rain's lashes
joining season's open cracks in the fabric of space-time
initiating contact with the ghost world, punishing mortal crime
burning fires extinguished in honour of Tigernmas, Lord of Death
rekindled by Druids from ceremonial flames, life-giving breath
darkness descends upon the land welcoming All Hallows Eve
fractured seam revealing wraiths, escaping
other world's disturbed weave
spiritual forces released, let loose upon the human world
Sammael, Dread Lord, leading his legion's black banner unfurled
Judge of the Dead, demanding instant justice beneath silvery moon
Storm God wreathed in blackening cloud extracting his boon
worshipping their idol Cromm Cruach, serving him fresh blood
human gifts at the feast of Samhain masked in sacrificial hood
skeleton spectres riding chariots adorned with victims' heads
their enemy's life-force dripping upon the ground in splattered reds
Albion's natives ruling blood and fear speculate by the stars
Cwyn Annwn, hounds of Hell break free their dimensional bars
bringing destruction to fear-filled forests in fading light
racing through countryside on this dark and desolate night
pursuing the souls of unshriven man and the unbaptised child
Gruacach and Balor of Evil Eye, mythical monsters running wild
'God of Death', look not upon his single, staring, baleful eye
for all who do will surely shrivel before him as they die.

Paul Birkitt

HALLOWE'EN

'Tis time for a greeting
Goblins, ghouls, witches and yes, living dead
Of a nasty 'trick'
Or maybe 'treat' instead
You look down at the children
Smile and give a sweet
Then you pack them off
In line so nice and neat
Largest at the back
In sizes they go down
Maybe say a tiny one
Just two feet from the ground
I mean by that from head to toe
Has fangs when turns around.

Michael D Bedford

THE PIANO PLAYER

Let your fingers play
the wonderful piano.

You know your music
day after day.

Each careful sound
Invigorates my ears.
It may be joyful music
Or music to reduce me to tears.

You're the master
of the keyboard.
A king of notes
to be assured.

You play with
such dignity
and, I am helpless
in your sound.
For as long as I
go on living
there is nothing
more beautiful
to be found.

David Charman

DRIVING

Driving is no pleasure on the roads today,
People drive like maniacs, stay out of their way!
Traffic jams and road works, a long wait at the red light,
Powerful, blinding headlights which dazzle you at night.
Cutting you up at roundabouts, jumping from lane to lane,
Drives on your back bumper, tailgating - it's insane.
Pinching the last parking place, it almost comes to blows,
A breakdown on the motorway, frustration till the traffic flows.
Driving behind a pensioner, when he's only doing thirty,
People trying to overtake, they really can get shirty.
Sign language and abuse; 'You idiot!' they cry,
Someone hogging the middle lane, won't move over - wonder why?
Motorbikes and cyclists, pedestrians unaware,
They're wandering all over the road, it *must* be a game of 'Dare'.
Small children when they break away from their mother's hand,
Be ready to push the brake down hard, or no chance will they stand.
Buses pulling out on you, 'Oh dear, missed you this time!'
Policemen waving you over, 'Have I committed a crime?'
Trying to read a road map, with one eye on the road,
A van in front or a lorry, carrying a heavy load.
Getting stuck behind a caravan, a tractor or a truck,
Getting caught speeding, on a camera, you swear, 'Just my luck!'
                              (or very similar!)
No, it's not very relaxing, there is road rage; it's them and us,
I think it may be more enjoyable, travelling by bus!

June Melbourn

A Giving Heart

A hand outstretched in time of need
A gentle smile, a thoughtful deed
The rarest of gifts come from the heart
Kindness is something we all should impart

We should all try to be more giving
Spreading joy is the key to living
Because when you give yourself, you'll find
A happy heart and peace of mind.

Gill Gardner

NEVER STOP BELIEVING

Count the way your blessings fall
each and every day
then you will find contentment
as you go along life's way.

At times when life seems pointless
or illness rears its head,
think of all the patients
who never leave their bed.

When you see a sunrise
or marvel at a starry night
then think how many people
never have the gift of sight.

Never stop believing
how fortunate you are
that you can lift your eyes
to see the beauty in a star.

When you feel downhearted
and truly on your own,
think of all the people
who live - and die alone.

So count your many blessings
each and every day.
Put your hand in God's hand
He will show the way.

Pauline Bloomfield

Wot

To quote a Morecambe and Wise term,
(Here are some poemswot I wrote,
There are only five I've written so far,
Are they worth a vote?
Do they have any scope?
Are they any good?
Dare I even hope?

Be brutal and honest,
Give it to me straight,
Should I suffer torture
Or some other dreadful fate?

I suspect they're terrible,
I only write them on a winter's night,
Well, I suppose it's better than arguing with the Missis,
And ending in a fight!

My wife's not too bad really, she's a dear,
After all we have brought two lovely kids up, to be fair,
Although she's suffered a bit from wear and tear,
That comes to us all from year to year!

She often says to me,
'You married no oil painting, Dick!'
So I just remind her,
'No dear, more of an oil slick!'

Persi-Vere

GAMES

I look to see the world in my confusion,
They look to see the world in their delusion.
I hold back with words in the illusion,
They move towards the words
With fusion.

I look to see the pictures unfolding,
They look to see the scene they are holding.
I can observe the changing with reason,
They only seem to notice
The season.

They seem to search to find their place,
I seem to roam to be out of the race.
They seem content with the life they see,
I seem to reflect for a space to be.

I can see the world of change,
They oversee the perfection and range.
I am happy to let it all be,
They are fraught
To chase and see

I can laugh and see life's games,
They will cry and remember.

Ricky N Lock

RIVINGTON VIEWS

Reservoir reflecting while relaxation
Images of wonders lighten imagination
Ventures reveal while admiring the views
Impressive sights for your eyes to immerse
Nature of plenty up here in the north
Gorgeous scenes of beauty and grace
Tea at the barn with cake to taste
Outdoor fun, a day so outstanding
North-west attractions to wander and wonder.

Laird P Brewer

TO THE NAKED EYE

She's sitting in front of a mirror.
Tears upon her face,
her deep brown eyes filled with unshed tears
building up over the years

She's washed her face of those tears
while she's at it, washed away those years
no trace of the pain she so expertly hides
no one has she in whom to confide

One more look into that mirror
the only thing to see her pain
straightening out, running a hand through her hair
knowing she'll be here again.

Emma Scott

ANGEL ON THE SIDEWALK

He watched her from the bar across the street
At the same time every day
Saw her push her way into the sunshine
Like an angel from inside a dark cloud

She would fight her way through the lunchtime crowd
To a sandwich stall, a newspaper stand
He watched her chat to the paper seller
About work, politics, the weather?

He wondered how he could love so much
Someone he'd never talked to
Love the glint of sun on her hair
The way she moved her arms when she spoke

And then, suddenly, she was gone
Lost inside that big black building
And he was left to stare into his coffee
To dream of the same time tomorrow.

Karen Smith

PETER KAY

Peter Kay, no one can compare
He is the best, a jewel so rare
Guaranteed to make you laugh till you cry
Talent unlimited, such a comical guy
He's just so great, so much happiness and fun
Recalling incidents of when he was young
The scripts of his shows make you chuckle along
I've heard him sing, he's good for a song
Life's adventures, whether new or old
Are very funny when they are retold
Watching him will give you so much pleasure
Peter Kay is the nation's treasure!

Anne Sackey

SERVES YOU RIGHT!

Where?
Where
Have you been?
You're very late,
Perhaps that's why
Your dinner
Is in the dog
Instead of on your plate!

Jacqueline O'nions

LIVE YOUR DREAMS

Live for each single day, as the future we cannot see,
Why long for yesterday? Let the past just be,
In the world today, is too much pain and sorrow,
And one never knows what will happen tomorrow,
To get in a boring 'rut', is so too easily done,
Life can be depressing, especially without any fun.

Don't put your dreams on hold, they won't wait forever,
Opportunities you will miss, by leaving them till never,
We all have disappointments, you won't know unless you've tried,
Make the most of your existence, don't 'flow' with the 'tide'.
Welcome life as it comes, 'it's too short' folks say,
Always try to be positive, and enjoy every day.

G Siddall

OUR CHILDREN

Their brilliance overwhelms,
their beauty astounds,
and their presence is wondrous.
Emerging from us, they are bound to us,
and yet they stand alone,
their eyes reflect the souls of family past,
and their gestures mimic the recent dead.
Our love enfolds them from the first cry of birth
and forever and always the sun shines from them.
We are dazzled by them, these creatures wiser than we,
who resemble us . . . but are unique,
who inhabit our homes . . . but are strangers,
their brilliance overwhelms,
their beauty astounds,
and their presence is wondrous!

Jean-Angela Smith

HALCYON DAYS (NOTTINGHAMSHIRE)

Halcyon days - the old Five Ways
Hardly a car to see -
Standing so firm like a sentinel
That famous horse chestnut tree.

Those were the days of stability
With Mother Nature all around -
When an Englishman's home was his castle
And the bobby his beat did pound.

Those simple days - those golden days
When happiness was *free*
And humans welcomed the gifts from God!
Like the old horse chestnut tree.

Mary Skelton

THE MAN IN THE MOON

The man in the moon is a friend of mine
I can read him like a book
I can tell if it is going to be wet or fine
Just by having a look

If it's going to be fine, he will be clear
Then again, it could be frosty too
If he is cloudy, oh dear!
Rain and snow and windy also.

He has been there since time began
And will always be a friend to man
When we get lost or tend to roam
His light will get us safely home.

May Ward

CHILDHOOD

One day when I was three,
My mom placed a baby on my knee,
What went through my mind,
Jealousy, hate and a love that's blind,
For years to come those feelings stayed,
We had fun with the games we played.
Remember your first day at school,
And me acting like a 'know-it-all'?
That day when I was three,
And you were placed upon my knee,
I was given a friend.
A friendship that'll last till the end
I had a baby sister
And I'll always love her.

Emma Scott

CALL HIM TED

He's a rocker - he's a roller
He's a jet-black stroller
He's a sleazer-geezer
Show-stopper - big bopper

In the fifties - he's the shiftiest
Call him Ted . . .
He's a jiver - dance floor diver
Chief rock 'n' roller - Mr Maloner
Blue suede shoes - Mr Blues
Tutti-frutti on a rutti
King of the drapes - king of the crepes

Call him Ted . . .

King Teddy boy. Oi! - Oi! - Oi! - Oi! - Oi!
Jiver- fifties survivor
Leather-clad rocker - DA shocker
Jukebox bopper - at the hopper
Drain-piper - all-nighter
Slick-lighter - fifties reviver

Call him Ted . . .

A Morris Minor - fifties diner
Buddy Holly - 'Good Golly Miss Molly'!
King twister - Brylcreem mister
Just call him Ted . . .

Greased black hair - knuckle duster
Fifties - extraordinaire - Elvis impersonator
He's a rocker - he's a roller

Just call him Ted . . .

James Dean - hard and mean
Pink socks - teddy boy rocks
Oi! - Oi! - Oi! - Oi! - Oi! - Teddy boy king stroller
Jailhouse rocker - knee-bone knocker
Fifties shocker - me old mocker

It's old Ted . . .

Eddie Cochran - jukebox veteran
Rock 'n' roll invasion - Harley Davidson
He's strolling - he's rollin' - he's bowling
He's howling

Just call him Ted . . .

Stuck in the fifties - he's pretty nifties
Pushing fifty - wife's called Betty
Don't mess with the Teds
Elvis isn't dead . . .
You got Ted instead

Dean Riches

A Mortgage, Credit Card

A mortgage, credit card,
A ball and chain a yoke,
No freedom life's charade.

A house, a castle, bespoke,
A joy at first a home,
A ball and chain a yoke.

For each a varied game,
With Pandora set free,
A joy at first a home.

The years become a sea,
A slave to future's debt,
With Pandora set free.

We spend and spend, regret,
The money-lender's dream,
A slave to future's debt.

We always seek the cream,
The money-lender's dream,
A mortgate, credit card,
No freedom life's charade.

David M Walford

Night

Inexorably the shades of Night
    move silently across the sky,
Silver-laced are the curtains
    as the pale moon ope's her eye,
Furtive enigmatic shadows
    creep in the woodland glades,
Screening the dark marauders
    abroad on their nightly raids.

Moonlight gleams on the waters
    of a ruffled forest pool,
Wildfowl fluff their feathers
    against fresh breeze cool,
The blankets of night dark and soft
    settle o'er the silence deep,
As on timorous feet the nightlife
    emerge from their daytime sleep.

With all-seeing eye, the silent owl
    swoops down on his prey
Which searching midst fallen leaves
    has no time to run away,
Fierce talons grip the quivering vole
    as the owl bears it aloft
As a wedding gift to his new bride
    in her barn nest warm and soft.

The silent world which Night provides -
    the world in which we dream,
Is a world in which terror rides,
    where the strongest reign supreme,
In the morning, the sun will rise -
    the moon be dim shadow in the sky,
We will not hear the pitiful cries
    of the creatures who were to die.

F R Smith

WAKE-UP CALL

Gloom on Saturday
tears on Sunday
hurry up Monday
this is how I lived my life.
Years flew - wasted life

Woke one morning
birds singing softly
shook the gloom off me
went to see what I could see -
- I didn't know me

Life waited patiently.
Had to find it
get behind it.
Never wish my life away
never waste another day.

This is real - today!
The only chance
to join the dance.
Time marches on
and then you're gone!

Greta Robinson

FREE AND EASY

In autumn breezes
When the sun shines warm,
The dragonfly
Is a beautiful sight.
He sweeps through the air
With joy and ease,
Skimming the flowers
And passing the trees.
He soars and he dips
With wings of grace,
A body of turquoise
Iridescent and bright.

Then joined by another
Their game begins.
Weaving and racing
Flight of fancy ensues.
Away with life's cares.
We are light.
We are free.
Now is the moment
Tomorrow is far.

For fragile is beauty
And youth is today
So live whilst we're able
In true
Harmony.

Lyn Sandford

WAR IS NOT FOR ME

I remember my prayers, the day before.
The day before I went to war.
Thank you God, for my life.
Thank you God, for my wife.
And all the things I had to say,
When I knelt down in the sand to pray.
War is near, for me, today.

Now here we are, with noise and dust,
To gain the Iraqi people's trust.
To help them live, without their tears
And give them hope, allay their fears.
That we will protect them, for as long as we stay.
War is real for me today.

The bullets rip, tear into flesh.
Arms and legs, give one last thresh.
Shells explode, the tanks on fire.
Heap the bodies on the funeral pyre.
And all around, the smell of decay.
War was Hell for me today.

Now the world is black as night,
For I have fought in my last fight,
And now beneath this flag I lie.
I feel no earth, I see no sky.
This is the price we have to pay.
War is not for me today.

Dennis L Vasey

THE FOG

The murky fiend from the subterranean
Surfaces to the human like a cataract,
Or a floating gossamer silk shroud
Manifesting as Satan's ardent friend.

Its mortality is often dependant on the falling evening sun,
It taunts us with its potent presence before suddenly it's gone.
The cruel mists employ a childhood game of hide and seek,
The vapours prey upon the vulnerable and try to trap the weak.
It craves the morning motorway for its horrifying stage,
Wretched tragedy not comedy is its favoured theatre set.
The offensive clammy veil begins but has no substance in its act,
The frozen tendrils beckon all the reckless to make their fatal pact.
The forbidden siren's repertoire it imitates to all who listen well,
Its elusive composition, a summons to respond to death's evil knell.

Heed me well you drivers,
Its reward is everlasting!

Lorraine Noble

POSSIBLE DREAMS

Back in the land of nowhere, in a place of make-believe
Where anything can happen, any notion you can conceive
Live in a fairy castle, with curtains made of gauze
Silver rugs beneath your feet, gold pictures on the walls.
Moonbeams that you can fly through on any starry night,
See the knights in silver armour, on white horses taking flight
Princesses with long golden hair, jewels on their gowns
And scores of little children tap dancing on the ground.
Goblins, sprites, elves and gnomes, all in brilliant colours
They make music every night, and hide inside the flowers
The land is called Tranquillity, it's there for everyone,
Best time to pay a visit is when sleepy time comes on.
Then you must leave behind, all worries from the day
Forget about your heartaches, throw your cares away,
Know that you are safe inside the Kingdom of the Free
A world full of adventure where mortals cease to be
Perhaps, when you awaken, in early morning light
Maybe you have forgotten, what happened in the night
Day will dawn, as now it must, you should feel at peace
This land of full tranquillity is seldom out of reach.

Joan Prentice

ODE TO SERAPHIM

Beautiful girl, that I did love, as sweet as music from angels above,
a soulmate, that you are to me, to love to live, for kissing thee,
nothing more that can be said, about above, so Heaven wed,
thee to me and me to you, what a blessing; love is true,
in my heart, eternal vow, speak the word. I do it now,
first rid yourselves of swinish sow, you may ask, you people, how?
Wisdom, Friend, so take a bow, astonishment, gosh and . . . *wow!*

C Thornton

Fireworks Day

My little daughter, with delight squeals,
There go some more Catherine wheels,
Whilst Terry, safely in his pocket,
Nurses a Roman rocket,
Soon the bonfire will be lit,
And the flames crackle and spit,
A day for the youngsters,
Then surely this is it?
Whilst I join the other funsters,
I think of the fun we had,
When I was a lad,
'A penny for the guy, Missis?'
As rockets levitate,
Oh! What joy this is,
This is great,
To watch the guy go up in smoke,
First his hat, then his cloak,
Another sparkler do I stoke,
And see my darlings' faces,
Surely there's no better places,
Than to be
Just we three
On November the fifth
At a bonfire?

Alan Pow

DRIVING THROUGH MENNA
(im Michael Woods)

The good day gone, I trail
a lorry huge as a house-removal,
remembering your late-spring swerve
on the big bend like a scimitar's fatal curve
cutting off your life's handsome head
with one swift stroke, your car striking you stone-dead,
crushed against the cob-walled cottage on the other side
of the road to Newquay. Your lonely ride
into death's dark leaves us all lost
in a limbo of loss, incapable of counting the cost
of someone like you, a gifted artist
and Land's End's resident sculptor, each wave's raised fist
roaring with revolutionary tides under a cloud-crowded moon.
Last night was like that, a black blanket of oblivion
stitched by stunning seamstresses of stars, such a sweet sun
promised by the light beyond the horizon's relentless rain.
I head home now as you never will ever again.

Roland Gurney

My Sin

I am poorly dressed and look quite thin
My whole appearance very grim.
I walk the street and knock on doors
To see if someone will let me in.

The night is getting very cold
As I rest upon a wall
And think about the happy days
Yes me, I had it all.

Good wife, two children, house and car
Good clothes and fancy shoes
Spend half my time in pub bars
And wake up with the blues.

I used to chat up local girls
And yes, I slept around
Now all the good things that I had
Are nowhere to be found.

Now I walk the streets down and out
That's repayment for my sin.
From street to street I knock on doors
But no one will let me in.

A F Mace

FAR-THING

I think, therefore I am,
I stink, because I can.

I enter the library, a restful place,
Well clear of the bustling human race,
Sit down at a table, mild and meek,
Then knowingly grin as I lift a cheek.

Both silent and deadly, you know the sort,
If whiffs were illegal I'd be in court!
Noses are twitching, looks coming my way,
My buttocks have worked their magic today.

Round from the counter with thunder of face,
No prize for guessing what she has to say,
'If you don't do whiffs then sure you can stay!'
Under my cloud I slope off in disgrace.

Nick Clifton

THE SNOW

The snow that fell so softly, while we were fast asleep,
Has covered everything in sight at least a good foot deep,
And now the virgin blanket's brought a fundamental change,
There's lumps and bumps and mystic bits, that all look very strange.

The sparkling, giant toadstool has a birdbath hid inside,
And leaning close against the shed, the bike I used to ride
Is now a snowy triangle, 'twixt white-spoked Ferris wheels,
And near the fence that Chinese hat my garden sieve conceals.

The birdhouse and the fence-post tops are wearing fluffy hats,
Except the bits, long since disturbed by the nocturnal cats
Investigating, in the dark, this silent white cascade
Which fell to Earth from starless sky, our gardens to invade.

Yet looking out beyond the wall, the fields are covered too,
In purest white, unmarked, except where fox has trotted through
With softest paws, and carefully, to reach the icy stream,
To slake his thirst, then hurry home to hide from full moon's beam.

The silence is quite absolute, there's not a single sound
From birds that shelter 'neath the eaves, nor mammals underground.
And we, in bed, cocooned and warm, will sleep 'til dawn's new day
Awakes us to a fairyland of white in which to play.

But, all too soon, the field becomes a playground, with a crowd
Of children with their sledges, and their laughter, very loud,
They build themselves a snowman, and then they knock him down,
And pretty soon, that dazzling white, is just a dirty brown.

The snow, and ice, on bough and twig, no longer gleams like jewels,
For snowballs have destroyed them - and the field's just muddy pools,
And though the children leave, at last, and peace returns again,
This snowfall's breathless beauty, will never be the same.

Geoffrey Leech

PARADISE

I lie on my sun bed on the golden sandy beach,
A tropical cocktail sits easily in my reach.
Far away from any hassle and work,
A relaxing evening and peaceful night lurk.
The sun beams down, its golden colour sprays,
Drowns the beach, where I currently lay.
The glass-clear sea gently laps at the sand,
I feel so relaxed and calm, yet grand.
Almost alone but for three or four,
This is paradise, I could not ask for more.
The luscious palm trees gently sway in the breeze,
Not a heavy wind - it is ninety degrees!
A plate of exotic and delicious fruits,
I begin to devour when me, it suits.
I take a sip of my pina colada,
To be anywhere else, I would not rather.
If I had the chance to relive this day,
You would know my answer; I think I can safely say.

Megan Strong (12)

RELAXING

The warmth from the sun penetrates my back
As I sit with my cat upon my lap
I'm trying hard to block my mind
Just a few hours to leave things behind

It doesn't always work, my chores to shirk
But if it's going to be a sunny day
I don't mind being up at five to iron that shirt
Then I don't feel guilty, if later, from the house I stray

The kettle is on so I won't delay
Make a 'cuppa' and I'm on my way
A magazine - sunglasses too - my needs are very few
Just one thing, I wish the garden had a loo!

Heather Moore

A CANAL LIFE

If I could take a canal boat
Sail from Land's End
To John o' Groats.
With ducks and swans
To escort me,
I'm sure I'd find tranquillity.
No radio. Just the birds to sing
Enjoying nature's blissful things.
No news of the day, my mind to mar.
No noisy horn of a motor car.
A friendly word to set me right
At lock gates painted smart and bright.
To moor up when I fancy so.
Take good food, then off to go.
I'd be the captain and the crew.
No one to tell me what to do.
I'd be a pirate, gallant, bold.
With treasure trove; jewels, gold.
Rest by pastures, pleasant, green,
Revelling, in the peaceful scene.
Stars at night, for company.
A canal life.
Yes! That's for me!

Bridie Sutton

Purpose Of Life

What is the purpose of my life
mother, sister or a wife?
I've tried them all and done my best,
but I still don't think I've passed the test.
I've done my best, I've done them all
but I don't think I've reached my call.
Now tell me what I should do,
to pass the test to please you?
I want to live a happy life,
I want to be a good honest wife.
If I do this and do my best,
will you please let me pass the test?
And then relief me of this pain,
and then everybody will be able to gain.
A good sister, mother and wife,
so I can have a good happy life.

Jean Hargreaves

DREAM ON

I live in a castle way out in the wild,
happier days, I am as a child.
Paint it a rainbow, colours so bright,
no room for darkness, only the light.

Dungeons and dragons you never do see,
but wild flowers, birds singing and beautiful trees.
No one else lives here, I'm happy alone,
just me in my castle, I call my home.

Doors I leave open, I'm safe inside.
No one to hurt me, no need to hide.

A princess I am, royal and free,
a beautiful robe and tiara for me.
Silk sheets, satin pillows, for me to lie on,
I lay down my head, and wait for the morn.

Suddenly darkness comes over me,
my castle is gone, only bricks do I see.
I open my eyes, a nightmare it seems,
No, I'm back in reality,
It was only a dream!

Mary McKeeve Moore

The Fourteen Million To One Chance

I'm a gambler, I'm a gambler!
Oh why do I gamble my money away?
Is it to fill my wallet this day, or is it because I want a holiday?
Oh what a holiday this would be, if only!

I'm a gambler, I'm a gambler!
Oh why do I gamble my money away?
One pound, two pounds, three pounds, four, five pounds, six pounds
                                                          sometimes more.
Is it because I need it for my honey, or what about my kiddie's tummy?

I'm a gambler, I'm a gambler!
Oh why do I gamble my money away?
Thinking to myself, no more I say, soon after I've thrown it all away!
Why did I do it? *Why? Why? Why?*

Was it for the dream holiday, or was it for the high?

I'm a gambler, I'm a gambler!
Oh why do I gamble my money away?
Is it because I'm lonely on this day, or is it because I don't care
                                                            for today?
If only I had been patient for another day!

The future has caught up with me, I need to face reality.
All my hopes are for my own family, that one day they will
                                                          understand me.
If only I had saved yesterday,
I could have taken them all on that dream holiday.

Now I have a new dream, it's a simple dream.
This is my dream, never to make false promises to myself.
Always facing reality, *daily,* to say what I mean, *daily*
And mean what I say, *daily!*

My dream is now true reality, as now I've got a close family.

George Petrie

THE CURTAIN SHOP

I adore your admiration -
The way you stop and stare,
Why, I can't think of anything
With which I could compare.
When I'm showing off my glad rags
I can sense each envious pang -
For you're in cotton, whilst on me
The lace and chiffons hang.
I'm posing in the window
For all to get their fill,
And I enjoy the smiles and sighs
And hold the posture still.
My dresser scatters flowers
Adding colour in array,
For what am I? A curtain rail
Emphasising his display.

Patricia Samuels

USA 1997

Jane and Jay had us to stay
We arrived by plane on a Wednesday
And had us a great holiday
Learning for ourselves, the American way.

Right-hand drive and *soopermart*
And Boulder Craft fair and Art
And new houses and garbage cart
And these were only for a start.

And for good measure, a grandson
Named Alex seven weeks on
He won the battle for attention
With vocal and decibel coercion.

All this in eight days
Following the American way
How Americans work and play
Birthright of Alex - if they stay.

Anthony Sherman

FRANTIC

Frantically wanting to get out of here
From this smoky, smelly atmosphere
Why this torment?
Do you hold the key?
Just get me out and set me free!
I'm gonna go out of my mind, staying in this place
Can't think no more
Can't you see it in my face?
This place is really getting me down
Cos all I do is sit and frown
This plea is straight from my heart
Get me out and let me make a new start.
I feel so sad and insecure
In this state of mind that's so demure
I need a little lift, maybe some divine intervention
From my guide or angel, all with good intention
I don't think I'm asking for such a lot
All I want is to be able to breathe
And live my life in a new house in a different spot
I know you know just what I need
So please listen and answer my plea.

Chris Needley

LOVER'S MEMORIES

Calm is the night, the moon is bright
Young lovers walk hand-in-hand
By a babbling stream, these lovers dream
In their own sweet wonderland

Under the stars in the velvet sky
They hope their dreams will never die
As hand-in-hand they stroll along
They watch the shooting stars go by

Born is the dawn so bright and warm
A new day so alive
The song of the birds as they fly in the sky
The humming of bees round their hive

These young lovers walk hand-in-hand
Beneath the blue summer sky
In their own sweet wonderland
And believe that their love will not die

Autumn has fallen and winter is cold
Yet still their love remains warm
These young lovers they may have grown old
But their wonderland weathered the storm

By the babbling stream these lovers still stand
Watching shooting stars dart across the sky
Love has not faded across the years
Though the seasons are many, gone by.

Tom Spencer

Darkness Embrace Me

Darkness embrace me,
Wrap yourself around me
Like a warm woollen cloak
And let me dream
Of liaisons by firelight
On soft sheepskin rugs,
The smell of mulled wine
Teasing my senses,
The flickering light
Casting shadows on
The chequered board of fate,
As his knight takes my queen,
Check mate!

A Vellam

SUMMER HOLIDAYS

Most people like a holiday, we've had quite a few,
Just deciding where to go is the hardest thing to do.
Do you fancy a trip abroad, touring, or by the sea?
Whichever you choose, it's certain, everyone must agree.

My hubby always let me choose, now which should it be
Guest house, farmhouse or cottage? It all depends on me.
I book the accommodation, wait for the postman to bring
The all-important letter, confirming everything.

I thought we'd try a cottage, I'm so pleased that we did
We always take our friends with us, we all saved several quid.
It was a little place in Wales, a few miles out of town.
I suppose that we were lucky, this one was not burned down.

Then we had a cottage in the Yorkshire Dales, comfortable, not small
Quite a tiny village, a church, one shop, one pub, that's all.
A small stone bridge was standing there spanning a tiny stream
With stepping stones, some ducks swam there
Nearby was the village green.

Some people like to go abroad, others prefer the sea
Some just like to tour around, admiring the scenery,
Others prefer the nightlife, the gaiety it brings
It's the little things give us pleasure, just the simple things.

We all like to ride around, going to different places.
Chatting with the people, seeing fresh new faces
Some we've never seen before, may never see again
But we still think of our holidays, the memories will always remain.

We've been to bonny Scotland, seen Derbyshire's peaks and caves.
Cumbria's lakes and mountains, enjoyed Norfolk's sands and waves.
The moors of Devon and Cornwall, Lorna Doone and Smugglers' land.
We've sailed to Jersey, Guernsey, the Isle of Man, the scenery
                                            was grand.

But when you're seeing these beautiful things, just remember who
                                                          put them there
And in the quiet of your room, just say a little prayer.
Thank Him for all His goodness, for everything you view
Is a 'Masterpiece of Creation', God's gift to me and you!

C M Thompson

Dusty Dreams

I loved you once in distant rooms
But time has got between
Stolen all that we once had
And left a dusty dream

A dream of perfect lovers
Burning in the night
Putting all the stars out
Surpassing all their light

You said for me you'd sacrifice
The child you longed to hold
Our love was much more precious
Than dreams you had of old

We had it all between our hearts
If only we had known
A stranger bearing riper fruits
Could take all that we owned

She beckoned you with promises
Of offspring that you lacked
The siren wailed, I felt you fall,
The ice beneath us cracked

You settled for a compromise
By drifting to another
You made what I longed for
Someone to call me 'Mother'

The child we failed to make you have
Your happiness complete
But she's a younger model
I never could compete

Thinking of her touching you
And guessing all you share
To know she breathes your sweet young breath
Is more than I can bear

In spite of all the years between
And knowing we're long over
By night I hurt with barren pain
Rejection now my lover.

Joy Pearson

WHO AM I, FRIEND?

I am an angel, shining oh, so radiantly true,
Sent down to show real love, just to you.
I am this very verse, that brings a sweet smile,
And helps chase away, those worries a while.
I am the very thought itself, within any rose,
With fragrant scent, and just for your nose.
I am also perhaps, a child, a father, a wife,
I am also the meaning, of your very own life.
I am also your rainbow, after any of life's rain,
Bringing colour to lighten, your sorrow and pain.
The very words themselves, you speak, as you pray,
And the strength deep within you, oh please hear me say.
I am also the sadness, within your sorry heart,
I will never leave you, we cannot drift apart.
I am also the drive, within your very own soul,
Helping, encouraging to achieve your own goal.
I am the memories right from your very own birth,
And I help you daily to show you, your true worth.
I will be there too, when you physically die,
But cannot then physically wipe any tears, as others cry.
I am who I am, and ask you, do you care?
But who am I? Look in the mirror, friend, your answer is there.

C R Slater

MESSAGES

I said: 'You look great with your glasses off.'
She replied to me: 'You don't!'

Roger had been dead a year to the day before he sent me his first text message from the other side.
The contact took the form of a poem which read:
'Fallen leaves like golden stars shine upon a dark green carpet,
fully fitted in the park.
Trees like rooted chair legs expose their thread-bare cushions.'
Typical Roger, he always enjoyed nature, and himself now buried in the earth.
His next message was a little more disturbing, it read:
'He's been looking for you all day long!
'Whom?' you ask.
'Why, the devil, of course!'
Did I mention Roger dabbled in the occult?
Of course I texted him straight back on that one, saying:
'Looks like he's found you, Roger! Happy Hallowe'en!' *Text 666.*

Vann Scytere

Hail To Thee 'The Enemy'
All's Fair In Love And Jaw!

In principal, we must be fair,
    When of a case we are aware,
That of kept women, we must allow,
    They fill up beds without a vow.

No matter if they be high or low,
    In course of time they come to know,
That passions cool, as time runs long,
    And love grows weak, that once ran strong.

To future times, they should perceive,
    When time itself their looks deceive,
As fair young maids, to old do turn,
    Their ardent lovers them do spurn.

This sorrowful tale is told again,
    Though only they will know the pain,
As from their warm and cosy nest,
    Their services are laid to rest.

When they grow old, and age sublime,
    And find they live on borrowed time,
It's best to take what's to be had,
    Although it leaves them very sad.

The moral is, if there moral be!
    There's no such thing as a royal 'We',
And when time comes for them to go,
    There is such a thing as a royal 'No'.

Toujour L'Amour.

E J Williams
A Bystander Poet

IT!

If you have it, then you earned it
Some don't have it, no doubt about it
Why not give it to another
A brother, sister, a mother?
Why not share it with the needy?
It is worth more given freely
If you have it you it treasure
Let another out there share the pleasure
If you can share it it is worth it
Someone out there does deserve it
If you can pass it to another
From their lowest they'll recover
While you have it it is precious
It is what the receiver treasures
It was given by He who dwells above
Is it what I think it is? Yes, *it* is *love!*

John L Wright

THE ANGLERS

It's Saturday, you know what that means?
They're off to plunder lochs and streams
Martin will drive
William to navigate
The sun is up
Let's not be late
They have their rods and picnic too
On cold days they have a barbecue
Off into the country to catch some fish
Then back it goes, never sees a dish
Will it be pike, carp or trout?
It doesn't matter as long as they're out
Maggots, worms, flies and lures
They'll catch a big one, that's for sure
The sky is dark, it's time to go
The photo taken, just for show
They come back home at the end of the day
And boast of the one that got away!

Linda Ross

MY GOD

I love Jehovah now and always
I commune with Him all the days.
He reveals His beautiful personality
Day by day showing His dignity.

My dignified God o'er all the Earth and sea
I'm happy to give Him my earnest plea.
For He is too, the happy God above
And sends His creatures all His love.

Tears of joy run down my face
As at His feet my words do grace.
He helps me through the challenge of life
Smoothes out the way, clears away the strife.

Denise Shaw

MERCHANT OF YOUR DREAMS

Dreams from the heart, bold and surreal . . .
Catch me unawares at the start
Is how they make me feel . . .
Dreams of every type and description . . .
You can find them in every type and description
Some are colourful, magnificent, simple or delightful . . .
Dreams are available . . . majestic or insightful . . .

Carol Olson

LIMERICKS

There once was an old man with a car,
Who swore blind he wouldn't drive far.
Yet he misplaced the brake,
Headed fast for the lake,
Then remembered exact, where they are!

There once was a lady with charm,
Who lived life on a dusty old farm.
She could never behave,
All-night parties and raves,
For the livestock that lived in the barn!

A lady once travelled to sea.
Gave the captain a nominal fee.
But with sickness went pale.
Out on the deck met a whale,
Who finished her off for his tea!

There once was a girl from Dundee,
Who stupidly swallowed a bee.
It buzzed round inside her.
So she ate a spider,
And then had fried chicken for three!

There once was a man climbed a tree,
Who said he just wanted to see,
The blue of the sky,
Then a twig in his eye.
His footing was lost, broke his knee!

Charlotte J Ireson

THE SHOPPING TROLLEY TWO-STEP

Down the central aisle we go into the middle with
A do-se-do
Now swing around and grab a can
Mind your step, you just missed that man
Now promenade down the second aisle
A pot of jam, that's the style
Mind them eggs! Well, never mind
I'm sorry, Sir, those remarks most unkind

No time to talk, it's on we go, to the centre swinging low
Potatoes now, fancy that. Sorry, Ma, if I've knocked you flat
Cabbage, carrots, lettuce too,
One step forward, then two back,
Reach the bottle on the second rack
It's fish for dinner and bread for tea,
It's time to step, it's a one-two, a one two, three,
I've missed the checkout,
Shopping, such fun, join with me in the
Shopping trolley run!

Gatekeeper

YOUR BIG MISTAKE!

You walked in my life out of the blue
After that all I could think about was you
Our love was a kind that is rare to see
Just where and when did you stop loving me?

How could you have been so cruel?
How could I have been such a fool?
You broke my heart, there was nothing I could do
I felt pain and hurt because of you

There seemed to have been no reason for your madness
And now it seems there is no end to my sadness
I missed you more than words can say
I think of you every single day

Seasons have passed and you're still in my heart
I just cannot bear us being apart
Now lovers may come and go
But these things I want you to know

I loved you like nobody else can
You were my one, my dream man
I would have done nothing at all to hurt you
And deep down inside you know that's true

I hope you find whatever you want and more
If not you may count on me, that's for sure
I'm now getting on with my life and new things
Looking forward to the future and see what it brings.

Some day I hope you look back and see
That that young lady was the one for me.

Emma J Riddin

GREY

Grey
The colour of inconsequential men,
Of meaningless pursuits
Wasting our precious time.

Grey
The colour of rain-laden skies,
Of dark ominous clouds
Pushing down on us from above.

Grey
The colour of roads and empty car parks,
Of endless miles of motorway
Urging us all ever onwards.

Grey
The colour of wood smoke,
Of surreal and misty mornings
Clouding our vision.

Grey
The colour of gunmetal,
Of weapons for war and destruction
Wiping out all our lives.

Grey
The colour of empty screens,
Of shadows and haunting echoes
Mocking our reality.

Grey
The colour of near death
Of grief and great loneliness
Leaving unrequited longings.

Grey
The colour of certain days,
Of negative thoughts and feelings
Nibbling at our souls but . . .   *Beyond and beyond,*
                                      The blue and the blue.

Denise Place

You're My Everything

You can cry on my shoulder
To shed away your tears
I will be your shadow
To hide away your fears
You'll feel warmer
And yet, a little bit colder
I will be your desert
So can you walk on my sand
And when the high wind blows
I'll be there, baby, to hold your hand
I will be your star
Guiding you low
Guiding you high
No matter where you are!

Anna Yates

LACK OF FORESIGHT

They have repaired the canals in Scotland
   and are boasting of the feat
But why did they let them die a death
   that modernisation could defeat?

France, Germany and also Holland
   have kept their canals alive
And with merchandise and tourist trade
   their waterways now all thrive

Britain did away with many things
   which she is bringing back again
It was lack of foresight at the time
   and history makes this plain

Our public transport was eclipsed
   the railways, trams and bus
Today they are spending millions here
   to give them back to us.

It was all about saving money
   through using different means
But for all their careful planning
   it has been smashed to smithereens.

Lachlan Taylor

NURSERY RHYMES

The men in Brussels
who flexed their muscles
ordering their schoolchildren to write,
nursery rhymes of today
knowing we would obey
as these would be read each night!

The oil in which our fish
with crisp potato crisps
had to be changed on joining the EU
Since then the following directives
which to the sane are ineffective
show what a stupid government can do.

Ring a ring of roses
now a banana poses -
a problem as they are not straight,
so off to the EU
to see what they should do
and many months are wasted in debate!

Our oak trees now offend
and we are told we must amend
our trees to please the German folk.
So off to the EU
to see what they can do,
perhaps Bonsai would please these nodcokes?

Italy's Willie Winkies
have small pinkies
and Durex for them are too large.
So off to the EU
to see what they can do.
Now Europe use two cut in half.

Newsreaders are too tall
so we must sack them all,
and replace them with those of smaller height,
so off to the EU
to see what they should do.
Dwarves or pigmies would suffice or might!

Do we live in a dream
or cuckoo land it would seem
when our MPs take note of this rot?
They say it is law
which the sane should ignore,
but alas that is what we have got.

D R Thomas

I'll Say A Quiet Prayer

I once heard a distant scream,
faint voices with no hope, no chance.
I saw a tear fall slow down a black cheek
through the biased pictures in a TV set.
I listened hard for a hope in hell
Through the chaotic hum of a digital age,
I heard nothing but an engaged tone.
Let me take you to a foreign land
where the water lies stagnant and brown,
a place were carrion lays hand in hand
with the forgotten children of our future.
It's hard to believe this still prevails
in a rich and prosperous world today.
I'll say a quiet prayer before I close my eyes.

Peter Wesley Hayward

INNOCENCE LOST

No swing, no slide,
For this child bride,
No play, no fun,
In summer's sun.
For it is the way of this girl's clan,
Who have arranged for her a man.
To him so soon will find her wed,
And he will take her to his bed.
For innocence lost I shed a tear,
And all the hardship she must bear.
I wish that I could change the world,
I would do it in a whirl.
But, alas, I know how not,
For I, too, am just part of life's plot.

Frances Ridett

MOONLIGHT

As I stare out of my window
I look up to the stars
I think of your face
I wonder where you are

I look down on the street
People walking past
The sun goes down, the moon comes up
And I realise how life moves so fast

The moonlight guides my way
To look for you
I follow the stars, to stop me feeling blue
Time passes so quickly as I think of you

For you are my world
You are my breath
Without you I couldn't be
So please stop my searching, come find me.

Melanie Rowe

BELOW THERE!

A lonely task, serving before the mast,
With little reward, for hours endured,
Protecting these sceptred isles,
World events will come and go,
But rest assured, there will be a stoker
                        down below . . .

A I B Vaughan

People

People are funny, I'm sure you'll agree
Of course, not referring to you or to me
At the crossing they look at the light that says 'Wait'
So they scurry across to the glares of pure hate

People are sometimes a very odd race
Like the drivers who rush to get three in one space
And they look at each other all waiting to see
If the other two idiots will move out for me

People can be most annoying I find
And in supermarkets the very worst kind
Are the ones grimly pushing their trolleys about
Up and down, round and round, and you have to watch out

For your place in the queue you can't leave for a minute
Or twenty more shoppers will swiftly move in it

People you know are a very strange breed
Not your folk, nor mine, we are different indeed
Take the ones who go off to the doctor each week
They don't feel too well and his advice they seek

After waiting for quite a long while to get in
They proceed to tell him how ill they have been
The doctor will give a prescription no doubt
Whereupon they will take half and throw the rest out

People amaze me when speaking of crime
It's of prisoners' rights that we hear all the time
And his reasons for doing the things that he did
Are usually blamed on his life as a kid

But, what of his victim? There's something amiss
When the honest are blamed while the thugs are dismissed
The people who puff on the old cigarette
They may seem quite harmless but this is a bet

If you don't smoke yourself, it's a blooming disgrace
When folk blow their cigarette smoke in your face
Well people are odd - they are certainly funny
I don't understand them at all
For if everyone did just as you do, and I do
There'd be no more problems at all!

Mary O'Connell

Why Poetry?

'But why write poetry?' one may ask,
'For isn't it just a thankless task?'
Oh no, indeed, it feeds the soul
And helps to make the spirit whole.

A poem inspires the spirit's mood
Which can transform one's life for good.
The 'music' of the words when read
Can oft remain within one's head.

One must have rhythm, also rhyme,
Augmenting vision all the time
So those who read may picture too
The image that you have in view.

Recall a scene within the mind,
Then strive descriptive words to find,
To capture essence of the scene
So it appears you've *really* been.

Expressed emotions drawn from life
(Whichever those of peace or strife)
In poetry, when by muse unfurled,
Can help your journey through this world!

Alan Wilson

ONE NIGHT!

My face is white, my lips are red,
Clothing and cape are soiled, ruined and ready to wear.
And just once a year, I can go out among the dead.
Wind is chilling, breaths are steaming, inside I shed a tear.

Children are knocking door to door for treats or tricks.
Their parents watch them carefully in case of trouble.
I float quietly past in grim attire as they get their kicks.
If they could see me, they would look away at the double.

I am a wraith, a ghost who is allowed to come out once a year, you see.
I am a wisp of fog or maybe a frog or the owl sitting in a tree.
I really enjoy my yearly excursion into the dark starry night.
And when you turn that corner, I just may give you a *fright!*

Helen Trevatt

SEASONS

Leaves, crisp, brown and gold

Unhinged to the ground
Never moving, never a sound

Unless a wind moves them along
This is Mother Nature's song.

James Patrick Milton

INTO THE RED SKY

Into the red sky, the migrating geese flew away.
They went above me, as I walked their way
The geese, dark silhouettes, against the evening sky.
I had to stop and watch them all, flying by.

Hundreds of geese, with their honking call.
Like the noise from a brass and rubber horn.
But these geese made such sad, soulful sounds.
Not as brash horns, honked by circus clowns.

They seemed to say goodbye, a long trip ahead.
Where hunters wait and so many will fall dead.
Goodbye to the summer, it's time to move on.
Flapping slowly, but the geese were soon gone.

Joe Wood

THE GREATEST SHOW ON EARTH

The poisoned chalice overflows, in a slowly seeping cascade,
And we are the daily bystanders to this constant daily parade.
Man's abuse of Mother Nature, our wanton misuse of her treasures
Now leaves us staring in impotent horror and seeking belated
                                            corrective measures.

We've poured all manner of 'Brand X' into the oceans and the rivers,
White foams and black oil residues, never asking the Earth
                                              to forgive us!
Colourless toxins and chemical waste, we've disposed of by the ton,
No one cared that maybe soon the Earth would glow like another sun.

'Roll up, roll up,' went up the cry, 'to the greatest show on Earth.
No admission charge, it's a free-for-all, only you can decide what
                                              it's worth!
See the incredible shrinking rain forest, it disappears before your eyes
Watch the giant hole in the ozone layer, and guess at its
                                              hidden surprise!

Be amazed at the political jugglers as they walk the tightrope
                                              of indecision,
Then hurl their ideological knives at the problem with
                                              incredible precision.
I'm sorry, we can have no animals in our circus anymore,
For the animals are slowly dying on the polluted forest floor.'

And still we pour more deadly wine into that poisoned chalice,
Polluting all we touch and leaving the fetid stench of
                                              mankind's malice.
Our world is slowly dying, and the future shall be the judge,
Of the species who turned the seas and forests back into
                                              primordial sludge!

So, roll up, roll up everyone for the circus of pollution,
More deadly in each and every act than any war or revolution.
And don't forget the clowns, every circus has its clowns,
We have clowns by the million, they cavort and dance as
                                        the planet drowns . . .

Brian L Porter

AT FIRST I LOOKED DOWN ON YOU, BUT NOW YOU LOOK DOWN ON ME

I first saw you resting on the shelf in the multi-store
'Hold on,' I called to me wife, 'there's something here I just saw,
Blister-packed, all neat and tidy, with price tag showing not too expensive.'
'O' come' she called, 'do not be apprehensive.'

Taking you home where I burst into the shed
Noting the instructions on the blister pack I read,
With trembling fingers the pack was ripped open
The little seeds were set in compost and watered quite often.

Each day I went down there to take account of your progress
At first nothing showed, hey, wait on, what's that, is it weed or grass?
So day after day, as I looked down, you flourished
The garden will be a picture if you are encouraged.

I planted you out when strong enough, by the conifer
Daily your progress was monitored,
Day by day down the garden path I sauntered
Your stem grew thick, your leaves expanded,
                    I had to keep you watered.

You grew and grew, I found some canes
To support and to keep you perpendicular during the rains,
Then flowers formed on every stem
Will the growing stop? I don't know when.

You carry on, four, five foot, six foot, seven
If you continue like this, you'll reach up to Heaven!
I count the buds on one plant alone, there are fourteen
Counted collectively, there will be umpteen.

So from those cold dark days of early spring
When I looked down you, enquiring,
To this bright day in September
When you look down on me, I shall always remember.

John Waby

THE MIDNIGHT CAROUSEL

In a long abandoned fairground,
Paint-peeling, litter-strewn
Rise a ghostly crowd of revellers,
Fog-born, within the gloom.
The carousel horses stand,
Time-frozen in their flight.
Until the whistle of the ghost train,
Chills this very special night.
Then the clock strikes the witching hour,
On church across the bay,
And slowly the fairground stirs to life,
A midnight game to play.
There's a creaking and a groaning,
The flickering of long-dead lights.
Whilst a steam organ coughs, then awakens,
Its music fills the night.
The carousel begins to move,
The horses prance with renewed joy,
To carry phantom riders; pallid spectres,
Ghostly girl and long-dead boy.
The swings, the dodgems, roller coasters, all,
In glory are reborn.
To cater for this spectral crowd,
Rages a distant thunderstorm.
There is music, long-dead laughter,
Through this late October eve.
'Til the fairground and the revellers,
Greet November's 'All Saints' dawn.
With the morning mist, the breeze stirs,
The chill wind bids them leave.

Jonathan Pegg

THE QUIET SCENE

In the loom chair where she sits today,
While idly brushing at her hair,
Gazing in the mirror, she scarcely
Sees the fittings, she'd chosen with care.

The luxury bedroom was reflected,
Full of the colours that she loved.
'How comfortable,' she murmurs
Still brushing her hair from above.

But how boring, nothing ever
Happens here, in this room, she thought,
Peering in the mirror, she gasps
Aloud, at the sight she had caught.

For in the mirror she had witnessed,
Not the familiar bedroom scene,
But another setting quite strange,
The most sinister one ever seen.

Terry Daley

LOST MY BOTTLE

Where did I put that bottle?
Was it the cupboard, or the fridge?
At my age I should know better
I really must think
My brain cells are dying fast
My memory just don't last
At this rate, it won't be long
My memory will be entirely gone
Perhaps I won't even know my name
Now that would be a shame
I could be someone new
Someone from the past
Maybe someone rich or famous
How exciting! I can be reborn
Some good must come out of this
Or will I live in ignorant bliss?
Only time will tell
Oh! What the hell!
Now where did I put that bottle?

Carol Hanney

The Fire Demon

Daring darting invisible demon, impossible to catch,
Ready to leap, running wild at the first strike of the match.
Arms stretching, directions diverting, awaiting to expand,
Dining, dancing, dressed to extend wherever reach is fanned.

Consuming fast and furious, tasting, licking with such might,
Hissing, melting, crackling, running over all that is alight.
Heat penetrating orange to flame, ease spreads to drying tinder,
Leaving only charred smoking waste transforming from each cinder.

Contained behind a metal grid pretending to be a friend,
Throwing out warmth to circulate enough eagerness to pretend.
While accepting each log in grasping gasps, the rewards gaining goal,
As flickering fervent content to welcome magic through the coal.

Courting, injecting each relationship transforming them to heights,
Dizzily dancing, sizzily trancing with energetic delights.
One rogue teaser twisting passion, like an overactive bug,
Seized by the demon, who feels defiled, then tossed onto a rug.

Singeing, smouldering, smoking, burying deep into the pile,
Furtively flaring through with flame, leaping to impress such style.
Alarm bells quiver as sprinklers deliver, doubting the moment's glory,
Until striking again! Who knows when? - Creating another story.

Peter W Hodgkins

Look At Me!

Look at me, I'm famous
An actress in a soap
But I find all this attention
Makes it difficult to cope!

I've got a brilliant story line
A really juicy plot
It makes me and the public
Think I'm something that I'm not!

I love eating out and clubbing
And really shouldn't pay
But the photographers annoy me
When I'm out shopping in the day!

The fans, they send me letters
They actually think it's true
It kinda scares me really
It's my job, it's what I do!

One day I'll get to Hollywood
There I'll really find fame
You'll see me on the big screen
The whole world will know my name!

Rowena

FORBIDDEN AS HE IS

I know this is love - this is it.
It's the way love is meant to be -
I will go through this, experience it
And inform my friends when they ask me.

I was writing the most important essay
When he rang and completely threw me,
I knew it could get messy
And that sick feeling began to stir.

'Are you on your own, can you speak?'
My body had never been so weak,
I could hear trembling in my voice -
I'd told myself not to speak to him again
But my body gave me no choice.

Over and over again, I'd ask myself the question:
'Why is it the person forbidden is the one
Whom you crave the affection?'

'It's just lust,' so they tell me '... physical attraction.'
- 'But I've looked at him eye-to-eye!' I've said,
'And I'm sure there was no reaction.'

'So why has he rung, as not much was said?'
'Hmm, probably bored before going to bed.'

But when friends are gone and no one's around
I know that it's me to whom he is bound.
The chemistry's there - I've never been wrong before -
Oh, it's killing me, Jonny - my brother-in-law.

At the end of the phone call I felt high as a kite,
For a moment I thought we had taken flight
Into a world where there's just him and I
'Yes,' my friend laughed, 'and pigs will fly!'

C Hansbury

WASHDAY

The washing is spinning full of glee
While I sit and watch with a cup of tea.
It's really quite fun to see them flirt -
George's shirt is groping for Amy's skirt.

And there go Minnie's ancient drawers -
She likes them long, down to her knees.
It makes her feel so much more at ease
Especially when she's out of doors.

As I still just sit and gaze
At vest and bra all in a maze
(Why Daisy sports a bra who knows?
She wears so little so-called clothes!)

Ah, there goes Grandma's camisole,
She feels the cold so much, poor soul.
But I see it's got a great big split,
I'll have to patch it up a bit.

Now here comes George's shirt once more.
He's flirting now with a pinafore.
He certainly won't get much fun from that -
He'd be better to try Aunt Minnie's hat!

Now Grandad's fancy boxer shorts
Are grabbing Lucy's minute knicks
They really must enjoy their sports -
Perhaps it gives them quite a few kicks.

Well, the show is over for the day
So I'll peg the laundry on the line
I won't put temptation in their way
Maybe they will meet another time.

Muriel Johnson

SORRY
(Dedicated to SR)

I'm sorry for always believing
What was strong inside my heart
I'm sorry for never seeing
The real you from the start
I'm sorry you couldn't accept me
And all that I can be
I'm sorry you tried to take away
What means the world to me

I'm sorry for always trusting
That you actually could have cared
If I'd have realised sooner
The pain I could have spared
Well my trust and love have disappeared
And now I think it's time
That I moved on and said 'Goodbye'
And spared this heart of mine.

Maria Jenkinson

OH TO BE AN ANGEL

I wish I was an angel
With a halo round my head,
But, in order to achieve this
I'd have to be - quite dead!

I have no wish to die yet
For there's so much left in me.
There's things to do and things to say
And much, so much to see.

I'll put aside ambition
For the time and concentrate,
On just doing, saying, seeing,
While patiently I wait.

L Alan Johnson

THE CHIROPRACTOR

The chiropractor is a manipulative man
He works all day as long as he can
Come in Mrs Hine - please sit down
Tell me your symptoms - that's a good start
Then I'll examine you part by part
Where's the pain - neck, back and knee
Don't worry about that
I'll manipulate all three
Please don't worry if you hear a crack
I'm only adjusting the spine in your back
It's been out of line for a year or more
No guessing why it's been so sore
Do you think I'm a physical wreck
Why do I have the pain in my neck?
I'll take an X-ray and have a peek
The treatment could start in less than a week
Frayed nerves in your neck from turning your head
It stems from your workplace - it has to be said
Lie on your back, I'll adjust the bed
I'll cradle my hands around your neck and head
Is the pain in my knee referred pain in my neck
Oh no, I wouldn't say that
You're just the proverbial pain in the a**e!

Marilyn Hine

SLAVE SHIP

The ship was large with a sail, nearly the size of a blue whale.
Handcuffed and beaten, then thrown down below,
I hit my head with a terrible blow.
Under the deck on the wooden floor, cramped together
you could hear people snore.
The floor is covered in poo and wee, this is the worst place I
could ever be.
In the hold it was dark with no light.
There was no day, only night.
People shouting, people dying, all the time you could hear crying.
For food we had porridge and water, I wonder what's happened
to my little daughter.
Finally our destination had arrived; the masters picked us in their stride.
I'm scared, not knowing what's in store, now I'm a master's slave
and really, really poor.

David Kolodynski

Our Village Green

In March bedecked with willows green
Weeping beside the passive stream,
The Green awaits beneath cloudy skies
For leaves to unfurl and sap to rise.

In gardens snowdrops herald spring
Robins, thrushes and blackbirds sing.
Naturalists begin recording
Where wild flowers grow and birds are building.

April brings cowslips on the field.
Ladies smock on the Green revealed.
Council grass cutters spare such treasure!
Leave our inheritance to bring much pleasure!

The carefree cuckoo sings in May.
Toddlers and grandads come to play.
Their daisy chains are worn with glee
For races, ball games and picnic tea.

All summer long, the children play,
Fishing nets, cricket bats and new-mown hay.
May fun and laughter always be seen
On our precious, treasured Village Green.

Doreen Lawrence

SUMMERTIME

See the swaying of the apple tree,
Hear the buzzing of the bumblebee.
Smell the scent of the flower bed,
Look at the birds flying high above your head.
Hear the children's laughter and fun,
Smell the sun cream as we lie in the hot sun.
Look at the water in the paddling pool,
Nice and inviting, clear and cool.
Hear the farmer ploughing his field,
Smell the fresh bananas that we have just peeled.
It's time for tea now so I must go,
To the bottom of the garden where only us girls know.

J T Lister

FOOD FOR THOUGHT

I live my life in limbo,
Until the thirty-first
Then the scene is set once more,
For me to quench my thirst!
Children in their masks and cloaks,
There's one with pointed hat.
Cries of 'trick or treat' I hear,
Beware the old black cat!
I roam the streets in my disguise,
With green eyes all a'glitter
Young targets are my preference now,
The 'aged' taste quite - bitter!
From house to house they wander,
With torches burning bright.
Quite unaware what lies in store,
This long and fateful night!
It's all imagination though,
I'm sure you do agree
So when they knock upon my door,
I'll say 'Come in for tea!'

T G Bloodworth

DOMESTIC VIOLENCE

Please can you help me? I've lost my way,
I don't know how to get out.
Can you hear me? Do you know I'm here?
I've forgotten how to shout.

You see every time I find my way,
Someone holds me back.
He teaches me to see the light,
And then it turns to black.

Each time I see if you will come,
And save me from this place.
What's that? Who's there? Please leave the light,
I'd hate you to see my face.

Jennifer Austin

UNREQUITED LOVE

Love is weird, love is funny,
You meet a lad as sweet as honey,
You think it's love at first sight,
But after a week you begin to fight,
You get married because you think it will bring you together more,
But finding you're three months pregnant, starts yet another war,
He wants an abortion, you want to keep it,
Later the baby is born, healthy and fit,
He leaves you in pain and walks through the door,
Saying, 'Go away now, I don't want anymore.'
Two years later that lad is still on your mind,
But he's in the past and the past should be left behind!

Stephanie Abberley

LONELY TEARS

What seems a long four years ago,
I was suddenly bereaved,
And I am sure no one can know,
How deeply I have grieved,
I woke up in the morning,
Beside my poor dead wife,
Who'd been my soul companion,
The reason for my life,
Some people think that I am brave,
While others say I'm strong,
But when I think about her grave,
Oh God, they are so wrong!
Ever since we've been apart,
Life's full of doubts and fears,
And no one sees my broken heart,
Or floods of lonely tears.

Matthew L Burns

Horatio Vincta

What do I see upon the line the ink would spill along?
This glimpse upon a lawless age that strains a modern song
What do I hear upon the tongue that entertains Jack Drum?
What trick of time delivers me to the verse that I have come?

Contemporary verse, this modern muse, it labours so my mind
Where little children, not amused, quote neither verse nor lines
No host of golden daffodils . . . no highwayman at night
No traveller knocking moonlit door . . . no tiger burning bright

No curfew tolling on the knell . . . no cornered foreign field
Or going down to the seas again to the tall ships that seas yield
No cargoes docked from Nineveh in England's April fair
Horatio Vincta has been seized and gaoled in Prosa's lair.

Calliope bide your muses . . . remember these sad days
For even father Zeus needs cry the death of Pierian ways
Yet I shall smile to forge such dreams on the anvil of my rhymes
For perhaps one day my children to mount and ride my lines.

M J Banasko

ICONS

They're more than mere celebrities,
these modern icons, quasi-divinities,
sacred personages, honoured by the multitude
with relative worship, your 21st century
equivalents of demi-gods and goddesses.

To be an icon requires one 'O' level
in geography or media studies from the local Poly.
Graduates need not apply. They're neither
Renaissance art historians nor brain surgeons.
They communicate in Strine or estuary English.

This one's a role model, despite a shortish fuse.
He sports, this year, a ponytail and Alice band -
in preference to the Auschwitz or Mohican look.
For leisurewear, he favours a sarong, his missus' thong
and bends his balls over the defensive wall.

This one's a royal fashion-plate,
self-pitying, self-absorbed and immature,
bulimic, anorexic, media-sly, her mediocrity
embalmed for ever in untimely death.
Uriah Heep, her butler, was her 'rock'.

This one's Australian with a modest voice
and general lack of modesty. She flashes
enormous molars and her cute, Antipodean bum
each day in each and every tabloid.
Her claim to immortality? That bum.

This other bum's more Afro-callipygian. A fallen idol,
fan of the former King of Jordan, the seven-foot
Negro billionaire, the basketballing star.
The more I see of modern icons, chum,
the more iconoclastic I become.

Norman Bissett

NEXT TIME

Breeze of salty air wafting,
Waves slapping soft on the shore
Twinkling stars in sky above
Lying on sands in your arms.
Today - from the depths of my heart
Thought about and well-savoured
Dusted down and then replaced
Until the next time.

Sheila Benard

The Fan

I stood there for hours
On a red-hot summer day
Amongst several thousand
Just to hear them play.

The hours seemed to last forever,
I thought it would never end
Then at last I was in,
And with the crowd I seemed to blend.

Waiting in anticipation,
Emotions running high,
Then there they were before me,
And I began to cry.

The beat just thumped right through me,
It hit me in the chest,
The crowd was going wild now
So I went with all the rest.

Lead singer walked towards us,
We all called out his name,
All the love washed over him,
It was his dream to have this fame.

It was over too soon,
Time for goodbye,
Took one last look at him,
As the lights lit the sky.

With the rock band gone,
The laser darts,
But the memories stay
Within our hearts.

Helen Carpenter

IS THERE A CHOICE?

Is there a fate prepared for me?
Will I be what I want to be
Just average and ordinary?
Will I control my destiny
Or could a greater power decree
What inner feelings I must obey:
Despite conventions of the day,
And latent desires aspire to convey,
A leaning that's inclined to gay?
Is there a choice? Will I have a say?
The words - I love - are so misunderstood.
From romantic nights to suety pud.
Love is a foreword for all that's good.
And as relevant now as in childhood
Is loving one's brother as you should.
But that love is sustained certainly
By a love that is limited sexually,
Perceiving cause for propriety
Respecting regards of society
And loving one's brother
With chastity.

Stan Coombs

FOOTING THE BILL

I've pushed them to the bounds of their support
and like true friends they've served without a thought,
they've given of their all;
obeying my commands without a word
both day and night, completely undeterred,
they're at my beck and call.

I must confess they have received abuse,
insensibility is no excuse
for ev'ry heavy load;
though overwork was due to thoughtlessness,
I made sure their appearance and their dress
were always a la mode.

Perhaps my expectations were too high
but circumstances often ruled that I
must put them to the test,
and sometimes I ignored their need for care,
instead inflicting further pain and wear
when they had need of rest.

Now I can only say in my defence
I never meant to live at their expense
and use them carelessly;
now I'm in pain, no doubt revenge is sweet,
I only wish I'd cosseted my feet
for now they're killing me.

Hilary J Cairns

ALTER EGO

Five letters spell my secret self:

T he
O ther
B eing
I
A m
S ometimes - Tobias

I am the baby caressed
at my mother's breast.

A child learning sums,
playing with my chums
at football scoring
goals and soaring
to the heights of fame.

At times, a growing boy
entranced in nature's joy.

Now and then I paint
for the family Medici
or become a saint
like Francis of Assisi
chatting with the birds.

Some days I walk
in groves with Plato
and learn to talk
the rhetoric of Cato
and for a while am wise.

Most days though
I hardly show
his side. So few can know
T o b i a s.

Anthony Brady

BEAUTIFUL AS YOU ARE

Why do girls wear make-up?
Is a question that I ask,
For all of you are beautiful
Why this need for make-up mask?

Do you improve on nature?
Is nature's beauty not enough?
For if you rely on make-up
You perhaps think that you look rough.

I used to wear a white shirt,
When I was courting in my prime,
And my shirt was caked in make-up,
When it came to parting time.

I said to my last girlfriend,
'What is the war paint that you wear?
And your hair that once was auburn
Why has it turned so fair?

But girls we really love you
For aren't you doing it for us?
And should your make-up look unsightly
Us lads won't make a fuss!

Gordon Barnett

HOME, TWEET HOME?

I'm the last little budgie in the pet shop;
A little budgie, lonely as can be.
I'm the last one on the perch, I've been left here in the lurch;
Just the cuttlefish, the millet spray, and me.

There was a dozen of us to begin with;
Some green, some blue, and one of us was grey.
How we chirped, and how we'd tweet! People smiled and
                                        called us sweet,
And most of us were snapped up right away.

But no one's asked for budgies since last Tuesday;
The kids all want a kitten, or a pup.
I've been on me own all week, and me future's looking bleak,
And I find it hard to keep me pecker up.

I wish I still had budgie friends to play with,
Someone to 'coo' in answer to my 'bill'.
I run up and down me ladder, but I can't help feeling sadder,
So I might as well just stuff myself with Trill.

I try to look appealing to the children;
I ding me little bell, and cock my head.
And I let them stroke my chest, and they seem to be impressed,
Then they go and buy a terrapin instead.

I wish I knew why no one wants to buy me;
A pretty boy I am, and good as gold.
Loving home is all I need, 'cause I'm slowly going to seed:
I'm the only little budgie left unsold.

Sue Coles

BLESS OUR DAYS

The gods are watching over us
Bathing in the energy of our love
Taking in the beauty and pleasure
From their kingdoms way above.

Stunned at our strength and endurance
Knowing that this is our own place
That they cannot keep us apart forever
For fear of losing their grace.

This place our own, they have no sway
My hands reaching out to you
Even in the mists of our dreams
Our hearts cried out for love true.

For we have toiled and searched so long
Knowing one day our love would come
From out of the mists of our dreams
To be together, forever as one.

For eternity our loves will entwine
No gods will ever encroach again
No more will our love be tested
Like before causing us so much pain.

Love has now passed its last test in time
To now nurture and flourish in all ways
Our radiant light will encompass all
The gods will now bless our days.

C S Cyster

IMAGES II (AZANIA)

When vultures tear the butchered skin and it is almost noon
When oxen float in formalin and it is springtime soon
When summer, winter, breaking fall adjust the southern dial:
Then scab-encrusted crones will rise and pass without a smile.

When coral spews its powdered plumes in black eternal fright
When rainbows stain the beggar's bowl it turns to miraged night
When birthrights, deathbeds, dying screams pre-empt cremation's pall:
Then fly-infested mouths begin to build a wailing wall.

When kudu kick the mangled thorn as grief o'erloads anew
When mako, tiger, hammerhead outstrip the ravaged crew
When worm-egged bloated limbs connect to tissue starved of care:
'Tis time to move to calmer times than these, or those, but where?

Victor Church

WHERE IS HEAVEN?

Where is Heaven? I do not know,
Where is the world where the free souls go?
Where are the angels, who help you die?
Are they living around us, or in the sky?
Where is the peace and happiness and love?
Is Heaven on Earth, or far up above?
Where is Heaven? Beyond the sea?
Where is Heaven? You tell me.

Stephanie Cox

A-Z OF ANIMALS

Ants crawl on the stair,
Bees buzz in the air.
Cockroaches I want to pound,
Dragonflies fly all around.
Eels electrify you if you're bad,
Frogs catch flies; when they get one they are glad.
Giraffes are covered with brown spots,
Horses around the farmyard trot.
Iguanas is a name I can't pronounce (!),
Jaguars on their prey pounce.
Kangaroos jump way up high,
Leopards have spots like eyes.
Manatees look like mermaids but are shorter,
Newts swim in the water.
Otters on the reeds they suck,
Platypuses look like ducks.
Q . . . I don't know; I'll leave that letter,
Rats run in the sewers and get even wetter.
Sea lions move their heads forwards and back,
Tarantulas are all hairy and black.
Unicorns have one horn on their head,
Voles have leaves for a bed.
Wildebeests charge around in the grass,
X . . . I can't think of; this letter I will pass.
Yaks sleep through the night,
Zebras have stripes that are black and white.

Mrinalini Dey

DIVORCE

All your lying, cheating, snoring
You turned out to be very boring
You were never true to me
It's for the best, just wait and see

I didn't want to marry you
But all the pressures forced me to
When I was on an all-time low
You filled my life with such a glow

You were on your fourth mistake
You thought your heart I'd never break
I guess it was a doomed affair
Cos my love wasn't really there.

You got down on your bended knee
I never wanted you to plea
I'm sorry but I have to go
Cos I don't love you, don't you know?

Carol Davies

SOMEBODY'S CALLING

There's a telephone ringing beside my bed
There's a choir singing inside my head
Is it a song of prayer?
Is it a song of love?
Is it past or future?
Is it all of the above?

John Faucett

A Day At The Seaside

We went to the seaside for the day
    Along the beach we ran to play
We built some castles in the sand
    Watched the boats going to far-off lands

We collected seashells on the shore
    The sand was hot, our feet were sore
So we went for a paddle in the sea
    Amidst the screams and shouts of glee

The sea felt good, but it was cold
    The waves were rolling big and bold
We went on a donkey for a ride
    We had to be quick, before the tide

Mum bought us candyfloss from a stall
    We sat and ate it on the wall
We sat and watched the tide come in
    And Mum said, 'What a good day it's been.'

Then she said, 'Put on your shoes and socks
    And on the way home, we'll buy some rock'
We bought some rock; just like she said
    Then home we went in time for bed.

L Fritchley

CELEBRITY STATUS

Becoming a celebrity is not one of my fads,
I would rather remain as one of the lads,
You see all these stars going out on the town,
Pretending to be letting their hair down.

Soccer stars not only behave badly on the field of play,
They are getting red cards for rape or fighting today,
So if the price of fame goes to your head,
Then I prefer to just take the wife to bed.

We have been married forty years and when we have sex,
We shut our eyes, I think she is Posh and she thinks I'm Becks,
Of course when we awaken we have to be quite frank,
We don't have their millions stashed away in the bank.

If people want to resemble the so-called stars in the soaps,
Then all I can say is that they must be real dopes,
It isn't really acting and the scripts are nothing but crap,
I'm pleased there is a switch on the telly, I can give it a zap.

Put all the soaps together in one show on one channel,
This way they would reduce most of the flannel,
For a title - call it the Street of a Thousand *********, or other,
Then toss it in the bin along with Big Brother.

Jack Edwards

BACKSTAGE

I am a singer
I sing the songs
I make the world sing
I right the wrong!

And when it's over
I get on my bike
Another stage beckons
Must take the mike!

Righting wrongs
And singing songs
'Til the day is done
Get my kicks out on that stage
Troubles have I none!

But now you're gone
And I'm alone
Every song I sing now
Has a hollow tone.

Adulation is a sham
My life's an empty page
I can't stand the loneliness
When I return backstage.

Stephen Friede

THINKING

It's nice to sit here
And think of you.
Thinking of the happy thinks
We'll always do.

Julie Wiles

The Day That You Left Me

The day that you left me
I remember it well
The rain it was falling
That day it was hell.

I sat and drank coffee
From a very large cup
I sat by the fire
'Til the sun came up

It finally did
I thought it would never
To know where you were
I would not know, ever

So I sat and thought
And I could see
That you no longer
Needed me.

Alison Mayo

STAR-STRICKEN

The great Professor Stephen Hawking
Lets his computer do the talking.
Incapable of even drinking,
All he does is sit there, thinking.

Chris Gutteridge

THE HATCHLING

You fell to earth from a mighty tree,
The Lord entrusted you to me,
I picked you up, you were so cold,
You were just one or two days old,
A baby hatchling I could see,
Another wood pigeon for me,
I am worried now as you can see,
Number two that fell from the tree,
My first wood pigeon is nearly grown,
I cannot turn him from his home,
He is too tame and thinks that he,
Is part of my family,
I made a nest upon my bed,
Not of feathers and twigs,
My duvet instead,
With tissues beneath him to keep him snug,
I would love to give him a little hug,
But I'm content to see him grow,
As this baby bird will never go,
He thinks I'm his mum like wood pigeon 1,
That I found in my garden when summer begun.

Ellen Chambers

CHANGE THE CHAINS THAT BIND

As I walk my road of life oft hear the clanking of a chain.
I turn to see who is prisoner, held down by chains of pain.
The clanking of the chain is loud, wondered who it could be.
Who carries chains that wear one down, have found that it was me.
The chain has wrapped around my heart and the weight has
                                                  bent me low.
Have found the combination that may help to let it go.
I must forgive my parents, forgive the siblings too,
Forgive all those who have hurt me and to me were so untrue.
I had thought that I had done that, alas, had just filed them away.
Once in a while I retrieve them and allow my emotions to have
                                                  their say.
This is a mammoth task for me, how do I let it go?
I've prayed to God to intervene and the way to show.
Bitterness, resentment, the 'buts' are my excuse.
These are the links that form the chain, from which I can't break loose.
'Thas caused a lot of scarring that can disfigure or enhance.
I'll change the chain into a garland and give to God my thanks.
                                                  Of course!

Rosie Hues

WHO LOVES - WINS

Reputation's everything, the ones without the sins
people flock to those who're nice, could say 'Who loves wins'
let them buy you, if you're such a good mate
many of the humble, will be made great
only in racket sports, can you do without love
there's nothing better, when push comes to shove
reputation's everything, the ones without the sins
people flock to those who're nice, could say 'Who loves wins.'

Mark Musgrave

My Guarded Secret

Invited to a party
People stood and stared
With pride I thought
I was the best dressed person there
I felt like a million dollars
With all the jewellery that I wore
And my clothes looked so expensive
Everyone loved and so adored
My guarded little secret
Kept under wraps so no one knows
From a jumble sale was chosen
Amongst the cheapest clothes
My jewellery from Woolworths was beautifully displayed
And everyone was fooled by
The efforts that I made
All lined up for fancy dress
Which one of us would win?
The judge's roving eye scanned over
Each one of us in turn
To be declared the winner
I could not believe my luck
My closest guarded secret
Never did become unstuck.

Joan Craven

FACING THE FUTURE

After the darkness, follows the dawn
And things can only get better.
After the long and lonely nights, when
You feel that no one cares and nothing matters.

Then one day the sunshine catches your eyes,
And with the passing of time it reaches your heart.
Cherish the good memories
Challenge your future and a new life will start.

Susan Haldenby

Rock 'n' Roll

You've heard about the whiskey
You've heard about the drugs
The endless nights without sleeping
the punters are the mugs

Genuine fans a-plenty
Stage-struck and in love
Their heroes give it all
In exchange for lots of love

The record companies line up
A media hype overblown
Four young lads line up
With no talent of their own

The media man says plenty
The boys are rather good
The management should know better
But the money's just too good

The press say they are stars
If they only could
Play a single note
Without taking a single drug

The pressure of their fame
Is clearly understood
The nature of the game
Their first show should be good.

Brian Lunt

Pain

I only wanted to be normal
I only wanted to be loved,
But the pain it just took over
It travelled through my blood.

The anger boiled over
It swirled through my veins,
And there right from that moment
I would never be the same.

The pain got to the heart of me
And turned my world around,
I couldn't make a movement
Could barely make a sound.

When I couldn't take anymore
And thought my life was at its end,
I was given the strength to carry on
And turned pain into my friend.

And there you are every day
Trying to gain back control,
But I will never let you back in
For I have courage within my soul.

Sharon Simpson

WHEREVER THERE'S A MOTHER

Wherever there's a mother, there is love.
She holds our dreams within her gentle hands.
When we are young we follow her with joy,
When we are old, she's our best memory.
A mother makes her little miracles.
She makes life sing in sunshine and in rain.
She makes life sparkle when her laughter rings.
A mother is the truest friend we have,
She's worth a thousand of our happy smiles.
She's worth each thoughtful thing we do for her.
The world is full of women, but we know
A mother is the Queen of all of them.

Marion Schoeberlein

A Sudden Storm

With sudden gust
The wind blew,
With forceful thrust
The storm grew.

With rhythmic drumming
The rain fell,
With ceaseless strumming
Around the dell.

With uncanny ease,
The wind dropped,
With gentle breeze
The rain stopped.

With strange silence
The wood was still,
With no more violence,
Save a slight chill.

With increasing heat
The sun came out,
With hearty beat,
The birds flew about.

Eddie Main

THE LUCKY HORSESHOE

The lucky horseshoe did not work.
It fell down on his head.
The doctor said, 'Another inch and I'm sure he could be dead.'
His wife, she was annoyed with him,
Because it had fallen off the wall,
'What if it had killed you, how would I feed these five?
That lump, it looks unsightly, but I'm glad you're still alive.
I'll write to the insurance company, to see if we can claim.
Where did you get that horseshoe from?
I'm sure you're not to blame.'
'My mother bought it in the market
And kept it in a sock, she hit a burglar with it
And she got an awful shock.
He took her to court for injury,
She was fined for committing a sin,
When she got home
She threw that lucky horseshoe into the rubbish bin.'
'So you decided to take it out
When you shouldn't have touched it at all,
Why did you stand below it,
When it fell off the living room wall?'

James Ayrey

ANCHOR BOOKS SUBMISSIONS INVITED
SOMETHING FOR EVERYONE

ANCHOR BOOKS GEN - Any subject, light-hearted clean fun, nothing unprintable please.

THE OPPOSITE SEX - Have your say on the opposite gender. Do they drive you mad or can we co-exist in harmony?

THE NATURAL WORLD - Are we destroying the world around us? What should we do to preserve the beauty and the future of our planet - you decide!

All poems no longer than 30 lines.
Always welcome! No fee!
Plus cash prizes to be won!

Mark your envelope (eg *The Natural World*)
And send to:
Anchor Books
Remus House, Coltsfoot Drive
Peterborough, PE2 9JX

OVER £10,000 IN POETRY PRIZES TO BE WON!

Send an SAE for details on our latest competition!